Pretty much everything you need to know about…

WORKING WITH 11–14s

'Tricia Williams and John Stephenson 2004
First published 2004
ISBN 1 84427 098 X

Scripture Union, 207–209 Queensway, Bletchley, Milton Keynes, MK2 2EB, England
Email: info@scriptureunion.org.uk
Website: www.scriptureunion.org.uk

Scripture Union Australia
Locked Bag 2, Central Coast Business Centre, NSW 2252
Website: www.scriptureunion.org.au
Scripture Union USA
PO Box 987, Valley Forge, PA 19482
Website: www.scriptureunion.org

Scripture Union is an international Christian charity working with churches in more than 130 countries, providing resources to bring the good news about Jesus Christ to children, young people and families and to encourage them to develop spiritually through the Bible and prayer. As well as our network of volunteers, staff and associates who run holidays, church-based events and school Christian groups, we produce a wide range of publications and support those who use our resources through training programmes.

British Library Cataloguing in Publication Data. A catalogue record of this book is available from the British Library.

Printed and bound by Interprint Ltd, Malta
Cover design: Phil Grundy
Internal design and layout: 3T Creative
Illustrations: Ian West at Beehive Illustrations
Photographs: Silhouettes of kids in motion, Rubberball productions copyright © 2002. Also Wild Associates.

Contents

Introduction

11–14s are riding the wave at a defining moment for faith commitment to Jesus – and it's vital we get alongside them as they seek to navigate the exhilarating, challenging and sometimes hazardous waters ahead.

As 11–14s begin to paddle out into the deeper water of independence from parents, the search for their unique identity is on. Are they going to be like their parents, or mirror images of their friends' values, styles and behaviours? What will they pick from the exciting range of options they see in TV or at the shops? The 'Who am I?' issue engulfs them – and brings with it loads of questions about life, faith and God.

Friends are major. We know that God thinks relationships are important too. Developing friendship with him usually starts through friendship with his people – young ones and adults. But there's a problem: loads of young people in this age group are giving up on church. How will they learn faith in Jesus if they don't feel at home around his followers?

It's easy to think they're a difficult bunch – no longer 'children', not old enough for the 'real' youth group. But if we wait until they are old enough in our eyes, we may lose an opportunity for a potential member of God's kingdom. They need to have their growing maturity recognised. They have loads of energy, love being with friends and having fun. They are honest, want to know answers and are ready for a challenge.

It can feel tough working with this diverse age group that has often been neglected and ignored by churches. 'Youth' has glamour; children's ministry has long-established respect. But 11–14s are at a fantastic moment for finding their true identity in Christ – and by the time they're 15, it may be too late. If your church is concerned about mission, encourage them to start with the 11–14s they know. This book aims to help you grab this opportunity – and privilege – and take up the challenge of working with God in their lives at a critical moment.

There's loads of information here. Try to think about it all in the light of what the Bible says. What questions does the Bible ask of the ideas in this book and the way your church works with 11–14s or about how we teach, relate to, and nurture faith in 11–14s? What questions does it raise for us about the nature of being an 11 to 14-year-old Christian today?

We've called this book 'pretty much everything…' because we're sure there will be something you'll want to know that we haven't covered. But we hope it will be a great help to you. Let's pray for one another and the 11–14s we know – that we and they will grow in faith as we work together in God's kingdom.

I planted the seed, Apollos watered it, but God made it grow. (1 Corinthians 3:6, NIV)

About the authors

'Tricia Williams and John Stephenson have many years of experience with this age group – both have been secondary school teachers, schools workers and are parents of teenagers. 'Tricia is currently the editor of *One Up*, Scripture Union's Bible guide for 11–14s and has an MA in Practical and Contextual Theology, for which she researched the role of the Bible in developing faith in 11–14s. She has also written books, articles and resources in the areas of Bible and faith issues for young people and adults. John Stephenson is Development Manager for Schools Ministry at Scripture Union. His recent research for an MTh specifically looked at using the Bible with unchurched teenagers.

How to use this book

We all learn differently, so feel free to use this book in a number of ways. You might want to read through the whole book from beginning to end, or dip in and out, referring to the chapters that meet your immediate need (although we hope you'll go back and read the others too!). We would encourage you to go through this book with other youth leaders in your teams. Why not use it as the basis of a series of training sessions for those working with 11–14s in your church?

You'll notice that the left-hand pages contain slightly more in-depth text, while the right-hand pages concentrate more on practical information and activities. These are designed to help you work through some of the issues raised on the left-hand page. Right-hand pages contain:

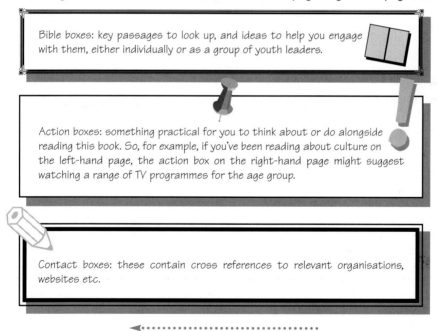

Bible boxes: key passages to look up, and ideas to help you engage with them, either individually or as a group of youth leaders.

Action boxes: something practical for you to think about or do alongside reading this book. So, for example, if you've been reading about culture on the left-hand page, the action box on the right-hand page might suggest watching a range of TV programmes for the age group.

Contact boxes: these contain cross references to relevant organisations, websites etc.

Chapter Link

Chapter links: to point you to other places in the book that deal with related issues.

PART ONE: 11–14s AND THEIR WORLD

Chapter One – Adolescents in the Bible

Why work with 11–14s?

Why work with 11–14s? We believe it's crucial. As we'll discover in the following chapters, it's a key time of life where identity is being formed and questions asked. If we are not there – showing 11–14s that the best way to live is Jesus' way, listening to and answering difficult questions, valuing their insights, walking with them through troubled times, sharing the love of God with them and for them – then we've missed a God-given opportunity.

> *Hurry … They are a field of ripe crops. Bring in the harvest! … Crowds fill Decision Valley. (Joel 3:11,13,14)*

Bible starting points

The Bible has a surprising amount to say to encourage and motivate us in taking up this challenge to support and nurture faith in young adolescents. But what could we possibly learn from teenagers featured in the Bible who lived in different times, thousands of years ago in ancient historical, biblical contexts?

First, God is the same. Second, human beings, including adolescent ones – even though details of culture and context might change – are the same too. Third, throughout the Bible, God encourages his people to build on his word given in the Scriptures – this is our 'faith story', showing us what God is like and how he wants to be in relationship with people. God's Word speaks into the very different circumstances in which we are living today, and those that will face the 11–14s we're working with now, in the future.

So, as starting-points for our thinking about how we collaborate with God in his work with this age group, we're going to take a look at the developing faith of three young people in the Bible. We don't know that all of them were definitely in the 11–14 age group, but they were certainly young and, probably, we would recognise them as being in the adolescent stage of life – dependent on the authority of others, but old enough to be out and about independently. See opposite for more about this.

Let's see what we can learn for our ministry with 11–14s today from Jesus, Esther and Samuel. As you read about each of these young people, try to keep in mind the 11–14s you are working with now, and think about what can be learnt from these Bible 'adolescents' to help us in our nurture and discipling today. Where better to start than with 12-year-old Jesus?

Think/talk about...

As you look at the Bible accounts of these various young people, think about:

- How are these young people like young people today?

- What factors in the young person's home/community life would have helped their faith develop?

- What role did parents and family play in the development of the young person's faith?

- What role did the believing community play in supporting the young person in their faith?

- How much does the Bible suggest these young people were involved in the worshipping life of their believing communities?

- What picture is given of faith moving from head to heart?

- What do the Bible stories about some of these young people teach us about the responsibility and ability of young believers to serve God?

All of the people in the Bible passages below were probably young adolescents – and they all had a significant part to play in God's plans.

They may not all have actually been aged 11–14, but given today's increasingly-earlier start of adolescence and all the clues in the Bible accounts about them, it's clear that they had lots in common with today's 11–14s. Read more about their stories in the Bible references.

Joseph (Genesis 37)

Miriam (Exodus 1:8 – 2:10)

Samuel (1 Samuel 2,3)

David (1 Samuel 16,17)

Naaman's slave girl (2 Kings 5)

Josiah (2 Kings 22,23; 2 Chronicles 34,35)

Jeremiah (Jeremiah 1:1–10)

Esther (Esther)

Mary (Matthew 1,2; Luke 1:26–56; 2:1–51)

Jesus (Luke 2:41–52)

The boy who gave his lunch (John 6:1–15)

Eutychus (Acts 20:7–12)

Jesus – the Son of God (Luke 2:41–52)

The big picture
The date is around AD 10. The Roman Empire extends around the Mediterranean. The land of Israel is occupied by the Romans. The Jewish people are allowed to maintain their own religious practices and beliefs, as long as these don't undermine Roman authority. For the Jews, their religious teachers, priests and religious rulers (Pharisees and Sadducees) are important respected leaders.

There is regular worship at the local synagogue, religious teaching by the local rabbi for boys, annual trips to major religious festivals at the holy city, Jerusalem. However, the Jewish people, living in their own land, are surrounded by the foreign culture and pagan religion of the occupying Romans. They are living in a plural society, much as we do today.

The wider community
Luke's account of Jesus' Passover trip to Jerusalem shows a 12-year-old who was well-loved, cared for and respected by his parents and wider family (Luke 2:40,52). His Jewishness – both nationally and religiously – was an unquestioned part of who he was. On this trip to Jerusalem, he was surrounded by his community of relations and friends (Luke 2:44). Jesus was part of a believing community, for whom regular worship together was an expected and enjoyable part of life. Perhaps his experience wasn't unlike that of the 11–14s in your group today.

Home and family
Jesus came from the small, northern Galilean town of Nazareth, although Joseph's family had originally come from Bethlehem, south of Jerusalem. Jesus, growing up in Nazareth, may have had the local northern accent. His family had a carpentry business. The Gospels make it clear that Jesus could read and knew the Scriptures well (Luke 4:14–21). He had been well educated as far as the social structures of the day allowed.

Whilst Jesus and his family wouldn't have been wealthy or prestigious, with Joseph's trade and business as a carpenter, they were probably not poor. At 12 years old, Jesus probably had younger brothers and sisters, mentioned later in the Gospels. His brother, James, would become a leader of the early church.

Jesus: growing up
When this trip to Jerusalem took place, Jesus was 12, the age when, traditionally, Jewish boys pass from childhood into adulthood. Like 11–14s today, he didn't want to be tagging along with his parents. On the annual trip to the big city for the Passover Festival, he was probably enjoying hanging out with his friends. The group, with its mixture of ages, would have meant his parents felt that Jesus was safe, sure that other adults were keeping an eye on him.

Then Jesus went missing. When his parents found him, there was a bit of tension (Luke 2:48–50). Then, as now, it's difficult for parents not to fuss about their adolescent children, torn between care for their safety and recognition that they are growing up, have their own ideas and are able to be more socially independent.

Think/talk about…

In what ways was the relationship between Jesus and his parents typical of that between adolescents and their parents today?

- What were his family and community like?
- How did he come to understand more about his relationship with God?
- How did adults help the young Jesus grow up in his faith in God?

Luke 2:41–52 Jesus and the Passover trip

Every year Jesus' parents went to Jerusalem for the Passover Feast. When he was twelve years old, they went to the feast as they always did. After the feast days were over, they started home. The boy Jesus stayed behind in Jerusalem, but his parents did not know it. Thinking that Jesus was with them in the group, they travelled for a whole day. Then they began to look for him among their family and friends. When they did not find him, they went back to Jerusalem to look for him there. After three days they found Jesus sitting in the temple with the teachers, listening to them and asking them questions. All who heard him were amazed at his understanding and answers. When Jesus' parents saw him, they were astonished. His mother said to him, 'Son, why did you do this to us? Your father and I were very worried about you and have been looking for you.'

Jesus said to them, 'Why were you looking for me? Didn't you know that I must be in my Father's house?' But they did not understand the meaning of what he said.

Jesus went with them to Nazareth and was obedient to them. But his mother kept in her mind all that had happened. Jesus became wiser and grew physically. People liked him, and he pleased God.

Youth Bible, NCV

Jesus' parents apparently protested because he had gone off by himself for three days without phoning (or at least texting!) to let them know where he was! Jesus asserted his independence from them. Their reaction probably included relief at finding him, plus astonishment at what they found him doing: talking to a group of people they were in awe of – religious teachers in the temple in Jerusalem.

Jesus showed the confidence of youth in talking to these religious leaders. Still, after this incident, it's interesting to note that he didn't make a break for all-out teenage rebellion, but settled back down to life in his home town, submitting to the authority, care and support of his parents for the rest of his growing-up years.

Jesus: spiritual growth

11–14s are at an important stage in discovering their own identity, a separate one to that of their parents. As we look at 12-year-old Jesus, the Bible account reveals a young person who is not only waking up to the fact of his transition to adulthood – with the accompanying awareness of responsibility – but also (excitingly!) to the fact that his true identity is found in his Father, God (Luke 2:49). This has special significance for Jesus' understanding of God's purpose for his unique life. Part of a Jewish faith community, he would have had 'head' knowledge of faith already, much like those in Christian families today, but perhaps this was the moment that he realised his true identity as God's Son – and faith moved from 'head' to 'heart'.

This moment of discovery has been prepared for by the nurture of his believing family and community. Adolescence is characterised by the need to ask big questions about life, and, for those brought up in believing communities, questions about faith, so that they can own it for themselves. Jesus is shown in conversation with teachers, asking questions and listening to answers in the temple (Luke 2:46); this seems to lead to an increased understanding of his own identity as God's Son.

Whilst the adults delighted at his understanding, the attitude of Jesus in 'listening' and 'asking questions' suggests a respectful submission to their authority. In spite of his growing awareness of his own special relationship with God, he deliberately submits to the authority of his parents whilst growing up – and whilst in their care, he continues to grow spiritually, which has an outworking in his life and relationships with others (Luke 2:52).

The role of his God-fearing parents is significant in his nurture. Mary's reaction to all this seems to suggest that although they didn't understand what was happening to Jesus (Luke 2:50), they showed a willingness to acknowledge something special was going on (Luke 2:51). We can sense their questioning about what God was up to in the life of their child and their willingness to wait, confident that God was at work. With our groups, too, we need to keep asking the question: What's God doing – and going to do – in the lives of each of our young people today?

CURRICULUM VITAE

Name: Esther

Age and date of birth: born in exile probably around four hundred and fifty years before Jesus was born. In those times, girls married young, so possibly a young teenager.

Next of kin: an older relative, Mordecai, who adopted the orphan Esther.

Place of residence: Persian Empire, far from the homeland of the Jewish community. Whilst they had settled down to life in exile, they still kept alive their allegiance to God, but their different customs caused conflict, and, in Esther's lifetime, nearly resulted in their massacre. Living in the king's household, Esther kept her Jewish identity secret.

Career progress: made queen, living in the foreign household of King Xerxes, which was filled with luxuries but where she could have been killed at any time. Enormous opportunities and power to work for God and his people through this role.

Faith development: continually supported by Mordecai, who reminded her of her allegiance to God and his people: '… who knows but that you have come to royal position for such a time as this?' (Esther 4:14, NIV)

Gifts, abilities, strengths: willingness to listen to her mentor; beauty, wisdom and great courage; took her responsibility to God and towards others seriously, in spite of risks to her own position and life.

Lifetime achievement: could have turned her back on God's people, to enjoy the good life – instead, her unselfish and courageous actions saved God's people. Esther used her gifts to play a great part in God's purposes for his people.

Think/talk about...

Brainstorm the reasons why Esther was an unlikely person to save God's people from massacre.

How are young teenagers in your church able to take responsibility in ways which matter for its life and continuity?

Samuel – called by God (1 Samuel 3)

The big picture

More than a thousand years earlier, another young boy, Samuel, was in the temple where God's people worshipped (not the same one Jesus visited in Jerusalem). The people of Israel were living in a troubled period after a time of leadership by judges like Gideon and Samson, when they were under frequent attack from the Philistines, one of the peoples who lived alongside them.

Later, God said to Samuel:

> *'… it is not you they have rejected, but they have rejected me as their king'* (1 Samuel 8:7, NIV).

How many of our young people's hurts arise from our society's rejection of God's rule?

The wider community

Eli was priest and spiritual leader of God's people. Yet God's people, including Eli's sons, were not following God's ways whole-heartedly. Eli's sons were exploiting their priestly roles for personal gain and sexual favours (1 Samuel 2:12–17,22). It was an uncertain time, both in terms of events in society and for the commitment of many people to God. Yet there were some who stayed faithful to God.

Home and family

Samuel's parents, Elkanah and Hannah, regularly went on the annual trip to Shiloh (where the temple was) to worship. Hannah took her longing for a child to God and he answered her prayer with Samuel. So, Samuel, like Jesus, was part of an actively believing family and community. Like Mary, Hannah acknowledged God's part in her son's life and entrusted him to God's service and Eli's care in the temple, visiting him once a year as he grew up. So, the childhood home for Samuel was the temple. His daily routines were bound up in the regular worship practices of God's people then: opening temple doors, looking after the building, regular sacrifices and festivals. Eli, his main carer, was elderly; his real sons, Hophni and Phinehas, were wild and didn't care about God or his people – so this was not the perfect family of believers. Yet, whilst Eli's sons had turned away from God, Eli himself had remained faithful, still listening to God.

For us today, there are few 'perfect' Christian families. As adults, we fail – and the young people we work with will have a range of home and family situations which are not always easy or conventional. Yet, we trust God, confident that if we keep listening to him, he will work through us to care for them whatever their home and family situations.

1 Samuel 3; 4:1 – Samuel – called by God

The boy Samuel ministered before the Lord under Eli. In those days the word of the Lord was rare; there were not many visions.

One night Eli, whose eyes were becoming so weak that he could barely see, was lying down in his usual place. The lamp of God had not yet gone out, and Samuel was lying down in the temple of the Lord, where the ark of God was. Then the Lord called Samuel.

Samuel answered, 'Here I am.' And he ran to Eli and said, 'Here I am; you called me.'

But Eli said, 'I did not call; go back and lie down.' So he went and lay down.

Again the Lord called, 'Samuel!' And Samuel got up and went to Eli and said, 'Here I am; you called me.'

'My son,' Eli said, 'I did not call; go back and lie down.'

Now Samuel did not yet know the Lord: The word of the Lord had not yet been revealed to him.

The Lord called Samuel a third time, and Samuel got up and went to Eli and said, 'Here I am; you called me.'

Then Eli realised that the Lord was calling the boy. So Eli told Samuel, 'Go and lie down, and if he calls you, say, "Speak, Lord, for your servant is listening." ' So Samuel went and lay down in his place.

The Lord came and stood there, calling as at the other times, 'Samuel! Samuel!'

Then Samuel said, 'Speak, for your servant is listening.'

…

The Lord was with Samuel as he grew up, and he let none of his words fall to the ground …

And Samuel's word came to all Israel.

NIV

Think/talk about…

What opportunities do the young Christians in your church have to share what they are learning about God with adults, as well as other young people?

Think/talk about some times when God has spoken to you through the words and actions of an 11 to 14-year-old. What impact has that had on your life?

Samuel: growing up

From early childhood Samuel, worshipped God and served him (1 Samuel 1:28; 2:18). Yet, we see that he didn't yet know God for himself at the point when the Bible shows him settling down for another's night sleep (1 Samuel 3:2–7). Just before the account of his meeting with the Lord, the writer of 1 Samuel records that the boy grew in stature (1 Samuel 2:26, NIV) possibly the 'growth spurt' characteristic of young boys as they enter adolescence.

Samuel: spiritual growth

Then, Samuel heard God speaking to him directly, by name, as he was lying in the temple. It was so definite that Samuel thought it must be his elderly foster parent. Eli, after the third time of being woken by Samuel, understood God was calling to the boy. This was the moment when Samuel met with God for himself (1 Samuel 3:7) – the moment when faith moved from 'head' to 'heart'. It's interesting to note that the elderly Eli did not doubt that God would speak to this young boy, but helped Samuel to recognise the voice of God. His modelling of submission to God as he heard God's message through Samuel, enabled him to teach Samuel about the kingship of God (1 Samuel 3:9). Eli's use of the word 'servant' (NIV) makes clear the purpose of God's call: it is to serve him. How willing are we to listen to what God might want us to learn through the words and actions of our young people today?

Although Samuel was young, God gave him a hard message for Eli (1 Samuel 3:11–14). As a young person, he was afraid of sharing God's words with a respected adult leader. Eli, faithful in spite of his failings, encouraged Samuel to say what God had shown him – then continued to demonstrate his submission to God through his acceptance of what Samuel told him (1 Samuel 3:18). Similarly, are we giving opportunity and confidence to young Christians today to speak about what they are learning from God?

This was the beginning of a life of conscious service for Samuel, as he developed into the leader of God's people (1 Samuel 3:19,20). As Samuel grew up in the temple, the account of his life suggests that he continued to grow in his relationship with God. No doubt, Eli stayed alongside, helping him to listen and understand what God was saying.

Whilst God's words to Samuel seem to have been spoken in more immediate ways than through written Scriptures, it raises for us the parallel of young people coming to know God today as they engage with God's words in the Bible and as they are helped by adult leaders to hear and understand. The subsequent chapters in 1 Samuel make it clear that the life of service God had called the young Samuel to wasn't easy, but it was significant in the history of God's people for their constant recalling to himself.

Models for today?

What's all this got to say to us for our work today with 11–14s?

- God works (often to significant social effect!) in and through the lives of young people (David, Josiah, Esther).

- Early adolescence is a significant time for young people with head knowledge of their faith to meet with God in a personal way (Samuel, David), for independent commitment (Samuel, Josiah) or discovery of personal identity grounded in God (Jesus).

- Just like young Christians today, young believers in other times have discovered that commitment to God means living differently to those around you, or in multi-faith societies (Jesus, Esther).

- Young believers in the Bible often grew in their faith during troubled times and in varying family circumstances: war, exile, without parents (Esther, Josiah, Samuel).

- Young people can take responsibility themselves and take action for God (Esther, Josiah).

- Immediate family or other primary carers, other believing adults and the young person's own believing community – all have significant roles in the nurture and ongoing development of 11–14s' faith (Samuel, Josiah, Esther, Jesus).

- Mutual respect and humility is required: recognition by adults of the importance of the young person's vision, spiritual insights and the ministry God is giving them and a commitment to a long-term nurturing of their spiritual development; submission by the young people to the authority of older believers and willingness to learn from their experience of God (Jesus, Samuel).

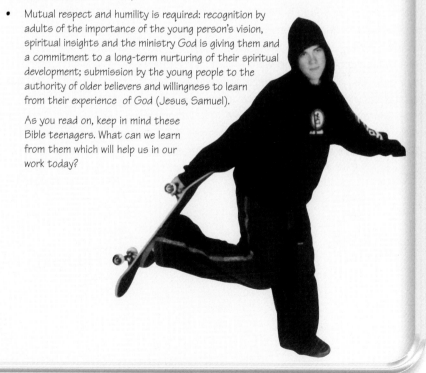

As you read on, keep in mind these Bible teenagers. What can we learn from them which will help us in our work today?

Chapter Two – the Internal World of 11–14s

Think about some 11–14s you know – for example, your group at church, the year 7s, 8s and 9s you teach at school, or your own children and their friends. Maybe there's a chatty, friendly boy who you'd describe as 'a child'. There are probably some girls, dressed in the latest teenage fashion, who seem totally immersed in their own concerns, and spend lots of time chatting and laughing together. You might have some increasingly spotty 13- or 14-year-old boys in your group, whose loud, physical, rough-and-tumbling and silly sense of fun might sometimes make you smile – and often stretch your patience. Then there may be one or two more mature, helpful girls who are considerate towards you and others in the group, are asking big questions about life, and are clearly growing in faith – and who wouldn't be out of place in a group of 17-year-olds. Other 'typical' examples will come to your mind too. How can you possibly work with these very different young people together in one group?

Children or youth?

11–14s are not 'children' – not in the way that 6-year-olds are, anyway. But they don't quite seem to fit the youth group either. So what are they – and how should we describe them? '11–14s', the age group description, embraces the English National Curriculum's Key Stage 3, years 7 to 9. From an adult perspective, thinking about biological development, we could describe them as young adolescents, this being the age group most likely to see the onset of puberty. The term 'tweenagers' is misleading because it can apply to children, who are clearly not adolescent, as young as 8. When big business uses the term 'tweenagers', it is often meaning children who want to look like teenagers and to whom they hope to market their products, exploiting this aspiration – more 'Tammy' than 'Topshop'. But these are often not the early secondaries who are at the beginning of adolescence. Neither would young people in the age group itself choose to call themselves 'tweenagers'. The word 'teens' is more informal, but not entirely accurate for a 12-year-old, and somehow sounds faintly patronising. This age group are also sometimes referred to as 'Mosaics', part of 'Generation Y', because their view of the world is made up of scattered fragments[1].

I praise you because you made me in an amazing and wonderful way. What you have done is wonderful … All the days planned for me were written in your book before I was one day old. (Psalm 139:14,16, Youth Bible, NCV)

What's so special about 11–14s?

Look at a selection of current magazines aimed at younger teens. If you're doing this with others, you could also have a selection of video clips of TV shows which are popular with 11–14s to get you thinking about style, language and popular values for the age group.

Now brainstorm in these three areas:

The world of 11–14s. What's really important to them (eg music, peer pressure, friends)?

The distinct characteristics of this age group. How are they changing (eg want more independence)?

Faith development. What's the nature of their faith (eg head, heart)?

Thinking of these three areas, what's your group like?

What should we call them?

Here are some terms which are used to talk about 11 to 14-year-olds:

- 11–14s
- Early secondaries
- Tweens/Tweenagers
- Key Stage 3
- Mosaics

- New youth
- Teens
- Early Adolescence
- Years 7–9

With other youth leaders of a group you are involved with, talk about…

- which of the above terms best describe 11–14s you know

- the merits and disadvantages of each of these terms

- how you describe this age group

- how you think the young people themselves would want to be described by adults

- a name for the 11–14s group at your church

New youth

However, if 11–14s are to be thought of as 'youth' rather than 'children', this term is too wide a category when it comes to creating targeted and helpful resources and developing practioner-expertise for the diverse age groups which terms like 'young people' embrace. Scripture Union, recognising these difficulties has suggested 'New Youth' as a way of referring to 11 to 14-year-olds[2]. This grouping, alongside 'Extended Youth' (18 to 21+-year-olds) and 'Traditional Youth' (14 to 18-year-olds), is an age group that until a few years ago would have been thought of as part of 'children's work'. Now, due to cultural changes and the fact that adolescent characteristics are displayed at an earlier age, the general description and category of 'young people' seems more appropriate – and, importantly, the young people themselves are more comfortable with this.

The difficulty in finding a term to capture the essence of the age group, which is at the same time acceptable to 11–14s, is not surprising considering its diverse nature.

Diversity and change

Diversity is one of the age group's defining characteristics and one of the big challenges in working with these young people. Their maturity doesn't depend on imposed neat divisions according to their ages, but on the rate at which they are growing up individually – physically, psychologically and socially. These factors, in turn, have significance for their spiritual development and we'll explore this further in Chapter Four.

It's also important to remember that whilst there are some typical characteristics of early adolescence, just as with older people, each 11 to 14-year-old is different and doesn't necessarily fit the picture. Boys and girls differ in the way they make relationships. Some boys, in particular, are likely to be much more solitary than girls – happily so. Some early teenagers love rough games, energetic activity and getting dirty, but lots hate 'roughing it' and physical outdoor team games. So, don't make assumptions on the basis of generalised characteristics, or on the one or two you know – or on your own personal preferences. In any case, at this age, they'll probably be completely different tomorrow!

This doesn't make for easy group organisation and planning – how can you develop a single approach to working with such a diverse group? Still, in a world which is never ideal, remember that 11–14s are grouped together in school and are themselves used to being treated as a particular age group. A uniting sub-plot for the young people themselves is 'change' – physical and social. They know it's happening to those around them and to themselves. And a first step towards effectiveness for leaders working with the age group is to recognise and remind themselves constantly of this key theme.

'Youth is better characterised by change than by problems.' Paul Fenton, *Someone to Lean On*

How is the above quotation true for your 11–14s group? Think about the young people you know.

- What are the changes they are facing?

- What difficulties does this make for them – and for you as leader?

- What are the good things that these changes bring in your discipling work with this age group?

Think/talk about…

- What are your own memories of growing up?

- Apart from physical changes, what else changed?

- How old were you when you felt you were no longer a child?

What's meant by 'Young People'?

The following definitions were suggested by Paul Fenton in Scripture Union's Youthwork Policy Paper as an approach to working with young people, aiming to contribute to good practice and to 'inform and set an agenda for strategic ministry provision'.

New Youth 11 to 14-year-olds	Traditional Youth 14 to 18-year-olds	Extended Youth 18 to 21-year-olds
These are the 'new youth'. An age group that 15 years ago was considered to be 'children's work'. Due to cultural changes they are now described as young people and display adolescent characteristics at an earlier age.	This is the traditional 'youth' age group and continues to display the most significant adolescent characteristics.	We can still describe this group as 'young people' and it is a grouping that retains many adolescent characteristics into the early or even mid-twenties.

Source: Youthwork Policy Paper, *Working with Young People – a Scripture Union Approach*

This chapter takes a look at 'internal' changes happening to 11–14s as they move into adolescence: physical, psychological, social. This is an exciting time of life. It can also be frightening and exhausting. It's definitely challenging – for leaders and their young people. And God, who made every one of our 11–14s, has great plans for each of them, and longs that they will grow into mature human beings who will continue to love and serve him through their lives. For now, our privilege is to serve God in his work, as we give support and understanding to 11–14s as they journey through this time of change.

Early adolescence

The transition from the dependence of childhood to the independence of adulthood – adolescence – is a particular challenge for our time and western culture. In our past recent history, when young people reached the ages of 13 or 14 years old, they would start work and get married – they were treated as young adults with its associated responsibilities. In the Middle Ages the extended adolescence we see today was unknown. In Jewish culture the bar mitzvah for boys at age 13 and the bat mitzvah for girls at the age of 12 has always celebrated the religious and legal maturity of young people. Similarly, in many cultures, the marking of the young person's transition from childhood to adulthood, with its new responsibilities, meant that one day the young person was treated as a child, the next as an adult.

Today in the west, partly as a result of our material wealth, we have a culture of prolonged adolescence, a stage in-between childhood and adulthood, in which physical maturing is not matched by the possibility of growing independence. Stress results from this when the young person physically and psychologically feels ready-and-able to accept responsibilities, but socially and materially remains dependent on adults. With the increasingly early onset of puberty, and increasing delay of independence until the end of education, this prolonged culture of adolescence creates difficulties for young people[3]. This tension is often reflected in our work with young people in churches where we also sometimes act as if physical changes are completely separate from the psychological and social ones (inevitably triggered by the biological). Take a look at the action box opposite for some examples.

Sometimes we don't recognise this age group's growing maturity and are reluctant to find ways of giving them responsibility within the church, or to take what they have to say about faith seriously. As in wider society, this can bring tensions and frustrations both for young people themselves and the adults working with them, leading to a sense of disenfranchisement within the church and consequently, maybe, to their leaving the institution of church, and sometimes, sadly, their disenchantment with the Christian faith itself. It is crucial that we understand and recognise the physical, psychological and resulting social changes which are happening to the 11–14s whose relationship with Christ we are nurturing.

Discuss these examples of the conflict between the biological and sociological examples of growing up. How might your church or group have handled each situation?

- Eleven-year-old Susan is now clearly a young woman. Yet her church group leaders continue to treat her like a child. Her discomfort shows in difficult behaviour. She copes by leaving.

- Twelve-year-old Chris is growing in his relationship with God and wants to go to the youth Bible study group – but the rules say he must wait until he's 14. At school, he leads a small Christian group. At church, he isn't allowed to make a 'real' contribution until he's older. By the time he's 15, he's lost his enthusiasm for God.

- Thirteen-year-old Amy is a really good drummer. She's encouraged to play regularly during church services. Gradually she gets involved in planning for worship services. By the time she's 15, Amy's life and relationships are caught up in the life of her church.

Thinking about adolescence

How would you describe early adolescence? Here are some ideas:

- 'If there were one piece of advice I would give to an adult embarking on a relationship with a young person, it would be that you should not see "adolescence" as a stage between childhood and adult life but, rather, as the very first years of being an adult.' Paul Fenton[4]

- 'A time of mirrors.' James Fowler[5]

- Explosion:

  'The characteristics of an explosion – its force, its potential for destruction, its raw power – are precisely those which are present at puberty.' Francis Bridger[6]

  Yet, as Francis Bridger points out, this is not an unexpected explosion. Parents and adults know what's going on and can build in safety valves.

- Chrysalis: 'It conveys the ideas of transition, growth and emergence …' Francis Bridger[7].

Physical change

The onset of puberty sets in motion a range of physical changes which begin the concentrated period of movement from childhood to adulthood. Little Joey is suddenly taller than you, and then there's the long-haired beauty (wasn't she the little girl with plaits and ribbons just last week?) who the older boys glance at with a new kind of interest!

Physical changes are the most obvious – although sometimes adults seem remarkably unaware that young people they've known as children are clearly becoming adults! They are also perhaps the most obvious changes to the young people themselves – and the most confusing and embarrassing. They need lots of discreet understanding and reassuring recognition, from adults, of their increasing maturity.

Whilst girls generally mature physically earlier than boys, puberty today in Britain can begin for boys and girls as young as the age of 8. For girls, onset of puberty is signalled by a sudden growth spurt, often around 10 or 11 years of age, by breast development and the beginning of menstruation. Many girls begin their periods and are wearing bras (and not just as an essential fashion item!) in the top year of junior school. The average age of the first period is now around 12 to 13. Boys develop slightly later, suddenly getting taller around the ages of 12 or 13. Around this time their voices begin to deepen, often made noticeable because of the unpredictable squeaking of the voice as it 'breaks'. Spots can be a problem as hormones are hard at work. You know your group best, but be sensitive – if you have a large group of 11–14s you might prefer to have single sex groups for this age group, making discussion and mutual support easier for those going through this stage.

Being sensitive

It's embarrassing to feel that adults might be noticing these dramatic changes or when peers comment on an individual's early or late maturing, relative to the rest of the peer group. The media's messages about ideal body shape and characteristics make all the physical uncertainties of early adolescence hard to handle too.

So remember

Situations like changing for swimming, or sharing accommodation for a weekend away can be painfully embarrassing if, for example, you are the first girl in your group to have periods and developed breasts, or if a boy or a girl is the last one in their group to be showing signs of physical maturity. Don't ignore it when someone doesn't want to change in a communal changing room – make it easy for them to have privacy. Notice when a girl doesn't know what to do about the unexpected arrival of a period. Don't fuss – but help her!

Be intolerant of cruel comments about other people's changing bodies. Words hurt. If you don't take action, you compound the hurt. For group conversations, try distraction, backed up with quiet reassurance later for the victim – but don't go on about it!

Positive energy – working with 11–14s!

It's great seeing the child you've known for years slowly transforming into an adult. What work has *God* got planned for them in the future?

- They are sociable. They love being part of a group and having fun.

- They can do more. It's exciting that now they can begin to be more independent and can look after themselves, sometimes without parents around.

- They love to take responsibility (even if it doesn't always quite work out how you'd like).

- On the edge of adult life, 11–14s' view of the world is widening – now they can get to know others, apart from families. Teenage friendships are a great place to learn about life – and God.

- They care about the big questions of life (more in Chapter Three). And they want to discover answers. What an opportunity to talk about God and his plan for their lives!

- They can be passionate about issues and endlessly curious about life.

- They have energy and enthusiasm.

- They care deeply about fairness for themselves and other people.

- Girls and boys of this age want relationships – with each other, and with adults, who are not their parents, as they begin to find their own way in the world. This age group is a fantastically rewarding opportunity for supportive adult leaders.

- 11–14s – because of all these developments – are naturally ready to discover God for themselves and their identity in Jesus.

Add to the list as you think about 11–14s you know – and thank God for each one of them.

Don't make assumptions that it's OK to talk with your group about issues of sexual development – check with parents/carers first. Some parents may assume that this is part of your role; some will, at least, want to be informed (as for school practice). Remember that individuals in the group come from different family backgrounds with different expectations of what it's OK to talk about. As questions and situations arise naturally in the group, be reassuring that physical changes are part of normal human experience and, for this age group, a common one. Help the young people to be sensitive towards one another, consulting and informing parents or carers as appropriate.

Although they need support, continuing to treat an individual as a child, when they are clearly now physically a young adult, can be hurtful, embarrassing and frustrating for them. It can be a difficult balance as you try to acknowledge their increasing maturity in the way you relate to them. Engage in conversation, invite participation, don't boss, don't patronise – and don't talk to them, or about them, as if they're a young child.

Change for these young people is not just about the physical changes. This growth is seamlessly integrated with other aspects of their development. Physical changes, inevitably, bring change to the way they think – about themselves, other people and God. This has huge implications for the ways in which adults must now relate to and disciple them.

Psychological change

Thinking

Puberty triggers key intellectual changes, as thinking moves from concrete to abstract. Now young people can think objectively about situations and reach their own conclusions. This is great because now you can get them to engage with issues – but they are no longer just going to accept what you say! They begin to reflect on what they see and hear. They can make intellectual and moral judgements. They will want to question and know what it all means. They will want answers to big questions for which you won't have answers. Their thoughts are no longer dependent on your thoughts, but are increasingly their own. Some psychologists talk about this cognitive change as the foundation for one of the central tasks of adolescence: the search for identity.

Who am I?

This is the big question for 11–14s. Until puberty, for young people brought up in a loving and relatively stable situation, identity isn't a problem: you are who you are in relation to others, you believe what your family believes, take your guidance about what is right, wrong and true from others. When puberty strikes, everything suddenly no longer looks so certain or simple. You begin to see yourself and the world from others' points of view. You realise that there are many ways of seeing the world, a whole variety of lifestyles and that not all families and communities have the same opinions about the right way to live.

How are 11–14s a different stage from children and a distinct category within youth?

This is the moment when…

- Childhood is left behind.
- Bodies change – dramatically.
- Thinking changes – from concrete to abstract. Now they can think logically, objectively, reflectively.
- Big questions of life hit them with intensity – as though they've never been asked before. They want answers.
- They discover their separate identity from parents.
- They want independence. Independence means the need for regular decision-making about how to live, when parents aren't around. However, legally, Child Protection Policy concerns still apply to young people under 16.
- Friendships and peer group take on major new significance.
- Relationships with adults, who are not their parents, can become significant.
- Older young people can be important as role models.
- New interest in 'image' is not just for image's sake, but part of exploring who your independent self is.
- Awareness of sexuality – brings new issues to their lives: identity, self-control, respect for others, right and wrong, with implications for independent, difficult choice-making every day.
- Whilst aspiring to independence, they are still dependent on parents – financially, emotionally, for safety, for support in interpreting the world and their new independent vision of it.
- Big questions mean questions about faith too. Faith needs to move from head to heart.
- This search for identity might mean leaving church and faith (many do – for a while).

The changes that are going on in the life of an 11 to 14-year-old are mind-boggling. But they are also at a fantastic moment for discovering God's love for them, his answers to the 'big questions', and who they are in relationship to the Christian family and in Jesus. Grab the opportunity!

Chapter Link

More about faith development later in Chapter Five.

Image

When you notice that one of the boys is taking a much greater interest in his hair than previously, or families find the bathroom is suddenly always occupied by a hitherto personal hygiene minimalist, you know that the biological time-clock has clicked on a stage. Suddenly the way you look becomes very important. James Fowler's description of adolescence as 'a time of mirrors' is a great image. The maturing 11 to 14-year-old begins to see themself with others' eyes – and they are often not very impressed. Having the wrong body shape, spots, the wrong colour hair, the wrong clothes etc can become a huge preoccupation when peer pressure demands conformity to your group – and the young person wants to conform because they want to be accepted.

But the right image is not, as Jenny Baker describes it, a 'one-size-fits-all hooded top'[8]. There are many sub-culture possibilities (get your 11–14s to tell you about the groups in their school) – each with its own fashion style, language codes, socialising, beliefs and values. Having the right image means inclusion for some and exclusion for others. During this stage and later adolescence, many will 'try' several different images.

For parents or leaders, 11–14s' preoccupation with the way they look can seem trivial. But it's important to remember that they're not just being difficult or silly. This is often a painful time for 11–14s as they find out who they are – and learn to love themselves, as well as others.

Sexuality

A central issue for identity and for this age group is their emerging awareness of their sexuality. Contemporary society's preoccupation with sex – for example, in the media and fashion – can add to the confusion which young people are already feeling about who they are. For most, they will begin to view the opposite sex differently. For those who feel that they are 'not interested' in boys/girls, as everyone else seems to be, there may be private anxiety about whether they're 'normal', or whether they're gay. At this stage of development, curiosity about sex, confusion about one's sexual identity or trying on of different roles are all common human experiences. It's an issue which will change relationships within a group as the boys and girls begin to feel differently about one another and suddenly find themselves self-conscious with each other. There can be much hurt about mistakes made and anxiety about things they're too afraid or embarrassed to ask. So adults need to stay aware of what's happening, to be perceptive, to give sensitive support – and always the assurance of God's love and acceptance of them and his readiness to forgive if they think they've done or thought something wrong.

Talking about sex...

FAQs and concerns are: How far can I go?; I think I might be gay; My boyfriend wants us to sleep together. How can I say 'no'?; I've had sex with my boyfriend. I'm feeling guilty.

Make sure that for any conversations with young people you are following your church's Child Protection Policy. Reassure them of your interest and concern, but don't get drawn into a conversation about sexual concerns on your own with a young person. Explain why a busy youth social evening might not be the right time or place for talking about their concern. Agree on some action – for example, getting other appropriate people involved, suggesting other sources of help.

Sexual activity amongst younger teenagers

Under-age sex is illegal – a 17-year-old boy who sleeps with his 14-year-old girl -friend is committing a criminal offence. But you might be surprised to know...

Research and surveys say...

- Britain has the highest rate of teenage pregnancy in Europe, although the large majority of teenage pregnancies occurs after the age of 16.

- In 2000 the number of girls aged 13 to 15 was about 950,000: 8,000 of these will have conceived.

- The above statistic means that in a school with a Year 9 (aged 13) of 40 girls, on average one will have conceived before the end of Year 11 (aged 15).

- Seventeen per cent of under-16s have had sex. Some surveys show a higher percentage.

- Research suggests that church-connected 11–14s are engaging in full sexual activity too, although the level is less for these young people than for this age group generally.

Source: Peter Brierley, *Reaching and Keeping Tweenagers*

Chapter Link

Read more about Child Protection issues in Chapter Eight.

For a few, this new awareness of sexuality becomes a focus of their identity and they may get involved in one-to-one relationships before we feel they're emotionally ready. However, for most young people of this age sexual identity is worked out in the context of a friendship group and this can be a great place to learn about yourself and about the valuing of, and your obligations to, others. A friendship group provides important mutual support through this stage.

All the 'Who am I?' questions can make life very stressful for the individual young person. However, whilst the hunt is on for identity, whatever the young person does, whatever 'image' they decide to try out, whatever unwelcome behaviours they get into, remember adolescence doesn't wipe out the experience of pre-adolescence. Whether or not it shows, what they learnt as children about right and wrong, relationships, Christians and God, stays with them. Their experience now builds on that and is shaped by it. So, how we invest in the nurture of children's faith is very important too.

Questions about identity don't arise for the child dependent on adults. It's as the adolescent strives towards independence that relationships with others, who are not their parents, become very important in their search for identity and purpose. This means change in the way they relate to others – and the ways in which adults, who are further along the road to maturity, must relate to them.

Changing relationships...

Peer group and friends

Peer group and friends now take over from parents and family as the context for finding out who you are and who you want to be. It's important for most 11–14s to belong to a crowd – although it's also important to remember that some young people are naturally more solitary. Being part of a crowd of peers is one way of establishing your independence from parents. It also allows 11–14s to 'try on' different identities: styles of dressing, music, behaviour, ways of dealing with others, beliefs and ideas.

Kelly is a typical 13-year-old. Most of her time at school outside lessons is spent with a small group of girlfriends. They talk about school, growing up, values and relationships. When she's upset by a bad test result, an argument, or an unfair telling-off from a teacher, her friends are really supportive and kind.

A downside of the close friendship groups amongst girls is the hurt which comes when there is a falling-out, or one is excluded – but learning to handle this is also an important part of growing up.

Mark, Kelly's classmate, also hangs out with a small group of friends. In contrast to Kelly's group, Mark's mates – all boys – support each other through shared activities (rather than talk): sport, computer games and music.

Towards the end of this stage, boys' and girls' single sex friendship groups tend to integrate, and as individual awareness grows, older teenagers are increasingly likely to pair up in boyfriend or girlfriend relationships.

Going out...

'In terms of sex, the only model we have to look at about teenagers and romance is the "choosing a partner" model. Many churches and Christian leaders are very firm that you shouldn't go out with someone unless you would consider marrying them. And that's absolutely right – if you're in your twenties. But what pressure if you're 13! ... for now, that's not even a question at all. Being friends is first.'

'An exclusively two-person team ... pushes other people out – whether that's boyfriend and girlfriend or joined-at-the-hip-best-mates.'

Source: Claire Pedrick and Andy Morgan, *Friends First?*, published by Scripture Union. Used by permission.

FAQs
- Is it OK to start dating at my age? My parents won't let me...
- I've not got a girlfriend/boyfriend yet. Is this OK?
- Is it OK for Christians to go out with non-Christians?

Talk/think about...
- What do 11–14s mean when they talk about 'going out'?
- In what ways do you think the boyfriend/girlfriend issue is different for this age group than for older young people?
- What are the problems for a group of friends when some of them start boyfriend/girlfriend relationships?
- How would you answer the FAQs above?

Find out more...
Claire Pedrick and Andy Morgan, *Friends First?*

Pete Ward, *Youth Culture and the Gospel*, Chapter 9: Sex

Before this, young people form groups and begin to go out together socially – to see films, to go bowling. It's fun – they are exercising some autonomy, experiencing some physical independence for the first time, finding out a bit more about who they are, without parents controlling how they are perceived by others. At the same time, the friendship group is providing some of the affirmation and emotional security that previously came from parents. And that affirmation comes from those who know you for yourself, apart from parents. For the young person this can be great, but, of course, there can be dangers too as the affirmation might be about behaviours, style and values we'd prefer them not to choose.

With independent relationships comes the burden of increased responsibility for the choices you make when out on your own – an important aspect of choosing identity. For Christians, central to our concern about their making right choices is our desire that 11–14s will find their identity in Jesus – as they grow in their understanding of their value in his eyes and choose to live in ways which please him. See Chapter Three for more on this.

Parents

Parents, and other adults *in loco parentis,* now need to keep a low profile around their offspring's friends and when venturing into their parent-free worlds (eg school). As a parent you are always in danger of being a source of embarrassment to your own children, no matter what you say, do or wear.

Through childhood until now, parents have been in control – what you say, where you go, what you wear, when you go to bed and get up, whether or not you go to church – and children have, in spite of the odd argument, not seriously questioned any of this. This dependence on parents, or other adult carers, has provided the security for the healthy and safe development of the child. However, with the emerging drive towards independence and finding their own separate identity, things change.

Now the young person has an irresistible instinct to establish a distinction between themselves and their parents. Consequently, parents can go through stormy times as their son or daughter challenges the boundaries hitherto unconsciously accepted. But be encouraged, having boundaries to challenge in the first place is important if this is a significant part of growing into their own person. Without them, they can't demonstrate that they are now ready to start making their own choices for living.

Arguments might be a frequent occurrence but the real reason for the squabble might not be the obvious one. An argument with a brother or sister about a 'borrowed' CD may be more about insisting on respect for separate identity and personhood, rather than really caring about the CD. Next time you're policing a row, look below the surface, listen hard and try to understand what's really going on. And if you can help the young people themselves to do that, so much the better!

Peer-group pressure

'What the gang believed, each member believed. What the gang did, each member did. Parents and school had to struggle to gain a hearing at all.'
Francis Bridger, *Children Finding Faith*, p98

Adults get worried about peer pressure, often just thinking about damaging influences. What do you see as possible results of negative peer group pressure?

Peer group pressure can be positive too. What might be some of the results of good peer pressure?

How could you contribute towards creating groups which provide positive peer group pressure for 11–14s – through church, in school, for social activities, for growth in faith?

About parents
11–14s said…

'Give us some space. Take some time in the back seat. You don't have to always be in the driving seat…'

'Don't always think the worst of me … or the best of me either! Let me be a bit flexible. When you've sent me to jail, and I'm in my room waiting to throw a double six, be prepared to sell me a "Get Out of Jail Free" card…'

'I want rules, but not too strict…'

Source: Claire Pedrick and Andy Morgan, *Friends First?*

'Parents must take a back seat. Those whose opinions are sought are increasingly teenage peers.'
(Francis Bridger, *Children Finding Faith*, p104)

Yet, this age group need their parents' support – even though they sometimes act as if they don't. In order to make wise choices, they need the boundaries which you provide – even if they do tell you 'everyone else is…' Practically, parents are indispensable at this stage. Apart from the boring stuff of how home and food are provided, 11–14s are totally dependent financially on parents. Unlike older teenagers, whose part-time job might provide income for independent local travel and a modest social life, the best a 13-year-old will manage is a paper-round (hard work, terrible pay!) or some occasional baby-sitting. Parents are also needed for transport – a particular need for younger teens wanting more independence in their social lives, including church activities. Whereas older teenagers might cope with unreliable public transport, many parents of 11–14s will want to make sure travel is supervised or provided by adults. Whilst older teenagers might be considered safe in a group out after dark, parents will want to ensure 11–14s are not out on their own.

There's lots of potential for tension in all of this. Alongside their growing desire for independence and aspirations to being seen as grown-up, 11–14s know that they are practically and financially dependent on their parents. Also, even though it might be well-hidden, they are still emotionally dependent on parents. Recent research has shown that 11–14s, in these significant years of development, still trust their parents more than anyone else[9]. Underneath any apparent rejection of parental authority and values, they rely on parents for self-esteem, emotional support and helping them to interpret the world.

For the parent, the challenge is to recognise the changes which are taking place, and to respond in ways which demonstrate respect for their child's growing independence – and support them in that. Take a look at the comments from young people on the previous page.

Leaders and other adults

Lots of the above will apply to adults working with this age group in other contexts too. If leaders try to act like a bossy parent, the young person will probably distance themselves from them too. Relationships with all adult authority figures will change, as the young person's natural impulse will be to question rules as they try to make sense of the world for themselves and strive to emphasise their separate identity.

The role of the leader of 11–14s is important, but difficult. With young children the adult's role will involve more explicit guidance; with older young people, the role is closer to an older friend accompanying them on their 'journey'; for early adolescents, the role is a mixture of both approaches. As for parents, it can be a difficult balance getting it right. Whilst this age like to know that the adult does have things under control, they don't want to be bossed around like little children. So the research in Reaching and Keeping Tweenagers suggests 11–14s prefer 'authoritative' to 'authoritarian' adults and 'companionship' to 'extreme control'[10].

Relating to 11–14s

- Keep communication open, allowing the expression of fears, asking of questions, trying out of opinions and the giving of support.

- Be ready to listen, before reaching conclusions or providing solutions.

- Help them grow towards maturity by providing choices and involving them in decision-making.

- Encourage them to take responsibility for themselves and others as far as possible.

- Increasingly talk to them as companions, not as subjects in the kingdom of grown-ups – a tricky one, as sometimes at this age you still need to judge when your 11–14 is really wanting the reassurance of the affection and direction expected in earlier times, or needing the protection of an authoritative voice when some clear boundary-setting is required.

- Respect/provide for privacy.

- Don't try to act like a teenager if you are not one.

- Be authoritative (you are the grown-up), not authoritarian.

- Accept and value 11–14s' friendships and relationships with their peers, young adults and other adults (eg teachers, youth group leaders).

Think/talk about...

- Do you agree with these ideas?

- Is there anything you would like to add to this list?

- How much is this a picture of how you relate to 11–14s you know?

Laura has loads of 'problems'. Leaders think she's attention-seeking. Laura thinks they don't care and young people her own age are too immature to understand. She's beginning to think church is 'rubbish' – when one of the older young people befriends her. Clare is 'cool' and remembers what life is like in Year 9 and how frustrating adults can be. She is also a Christian. She listens to Laura, takes her concerns seriously and encourages Laura to start praying about some of her worries...

Older young people, as mentoring schemes in schools recognise, can be significant leaders for younger teenagers. The older teenager doesn't have the barrier of 'authority figure' to overcome; they fulfil the aspirations which 11–14s have of being 'grown-up' and young; dress and language aren't a problem; they know what life for young people today is like; they remember the frustrations of adult 'control'; and if they also have a lively, growing faith, it helps the 11 to 14-year-old feel – at a time when they might be questioning this – that being a Christian is OK.

In spite of the difficulties of how leadership roles are worked out, this age group value and want relationships with older people – where they feel respected, valued and understood. Whilst the young person's drive to achieve autonomy will change relationships with adults, they, nevertheless, have an important role as facilitators in the process of growing up, through dialogue, through providing information, as role models and in stimulating exploration of beliefs and values[11]. Paul Fenton in his book *Someone to Lean On*, emphasises the simple need to accompany young people as they grow, making the point that many of the issues they are facing for the first time in life are, after all, some of the ones we struggle with too.

Stress and strife?

Adolescence feels like this sometimes – for the young people anyway. Physical, psychological and social development can bring hurt, frustration, loneliness, rebelliousness, isolation from adult support, doubts and uncertainty.

In this chapter we've looked at the internal world of 11–14s. There is no one stereotype that fits them all – a characteristic of the age group is their diversity. Life for them is all about change – very big changes, which involve confronting big questions about who they are, who they want to be and how they are going to live. All these changes bring social changes to the way they see others and the way others see them. Relationships with adults are changing. Peer group and friends become very important. Emotions are up and down. Then there is the special frustration of our contemporary situation with young people maturing earlier physically, but being dependent on adults longer. Being adolescent is a rollercoaster ride – exciting, but highly anxiety-inducing. In spite of all the challenges there are loads of good things too.

The great thing is that 11–14s – because of all these developments – are naturally ready to discover God for themselves and their identity in Jesus.

How much is your thinking in the areas discussed in this chapter informed by God's words? How much would your answers to young people's questions reflect what the Bible says?

Here are some starting-points for getting a biblical viewpoint:

- Growing up: Psalm 139:13–16
- Diversity: Genesis 1; Romans 14:1–8; 1 Corinthians 12:12–31
- Change and uncertainty: Joshua 1:1–9; Jeremiah 29:11; Romans 8:28
- Sexuality: Genesis 2:21–24; Exodus 20:14; Song of Solomon; Galatians 5:16–25; Colossians 3:1–17; 1 John 1:9
- Identity: Ephesians 1:3–14; Romans 8:28–30
- Image: Genesis 1:27; 1 Samuel 16:7; Matthew 6:25–34
- Friends: Proverbs 17:17; 22:24,25; 27:6
- Parents: Exodus 20:12; Ephesians 6:1–4

References for Chapter Two

1   Peter Brierley, *Reaching and Keeping Tweenagers*, p9
2   Paul Fenton, 'Youthwork Policy Paper'
3   Paul Fenton, *Someone to Lean On*, p34
4   Paul Fenton, ibid, pp34, 35
5   James Fowler, *Stages of Faith*, p151
6   Francis Bridger, *Children Finding Faith*, p102
7   Francis Bridger, ibid
8   Jenny Baker, 'Growing Pains'
9   Peter Brierley, ibid, pp2223
10 Peter Brierley, ibid, p36
11 John Head, *Working with Adolescents* pp5, 23

Further reading

Graham Cray, *Postmodern Culture and Youth Discipleship*

Claire Pedrick and Andy Morgan, *Friends First?*

Chapter Three – the External World of 11–14s

'Who am I?' is not the only question confronting 11–14s as they stand at the edge of adulthood. Growing up is also about: 'Who should I become?' Alongside the internal factors at work in 11–14s, there are the external ones which shape their lives and inevitably influence their search for identity.

Peer pressure is a major force on young people to conform to how others are living. But today, 'peer pressure' isn't easy to define or limit. Which peer pressure? There are many different sub-cultures, different values, different cultures – all at work in the big 'story' of our world, through the different people we live with, and through things like TV and the web. The problem more often has to do with making right choices. In any case, whilst 'peer pressure' sounds like bad news to anxious Christian adults, it can be positive – as young people with a different 'story' infiltrate the world, far more thoroughly than most Christian adults are able to do.

Some of the 'shaping' factors discussed in this chapter are simply part of what it means to live in western society today; and some depend on choices made by the young people themselves or their adult carers. These factors are all huge issues. This chapter aims to give a brief taster to get you thinking about what it's like being an 11 to 14-year-old in today's world. If you want to find out more, take a look at some of the books mentioned throughout and at the end of this chapter.

First, this chapter looks at: the big picture of what it means to live in the plural world of today with its mixture of ethnicity and faiths, questions of truth and authority, questions about right and wrong; views about sexuality; then, the contexts where young people live out their daily lives in relationship with others – youth culture, school and home and family. In the last section, the chapter looks at other external factors which are shaping the lives of 11–14s, which are all part of the 'self-selection' world in which they are growing up, with its emphasis on the here-and-now, including: consumerism, media, music and the impact of electronic communications.

Finally, there's a brief look at the question of how much all of these factors are forming Christian young people and the potential for them to act as transforming agents in their networks as we encourage them to live out the counter-story of faith in Jesus.

Life today...

Here are some words and phrases sometimes used in descriptions of life today:

- Uncertainty
- Individualism
- Fragmented
- Choice
- Imagination
- Story
- Immediate/now
- Identity

- Freedom
- Feelings
- Consumerism
- Image
- Spirituality
- Global
- Visual

- Think about each word/phrase. Can you come up with some examples from life today that fit the word? Now think of some which 11–14s are likely to encounter.

- Flick through some teen magazines (eg *Bliss, Mizz, Sugar*). Look for some examples which fit each of the above descriptions of twenty-first-century life.

- What does the Bible and Christian faith have to say about each of these? It's not all bad!

- How is the world of 11–14s today different from the world in which you grew up?

Whose authority?

11–14s are moving out from their parents' authority. But what/who are they going to put in the parents' place as the authority for knowing who they are, what they want to become, and how they should live?

Think about the verse from Judges below and what it suggests about the relationship between authority and knowing how to live with others.

In those days Israel wasn't ruled by a king, and everyone did what they thought was right. (Judges 21:25)

Life in a plural world

Diversity and choice

There used to be one big unifying 'story' (or metanarrative) in the western world, within which local communities worked out their own way of doing things – the Christian faith. This was broadly accepted as the authoritative basis for right and wrong, affecting everything from law-making to personal relationships. There was a shared value system. Today, that's not the case.

Every day, young people move between, and are shaped by, different groups and cultures, for example: home and family, school, the neighbourhood, church, web and email networks, groups and cultures suggested by the media. Then, there is the huge diversity of ethnic and faith groups in Britain today – and these bring with them different cultures and ideas about right and wrong. The young person has to struggle to make sense of who they are in the context of all these different elements. Diversity and choice, whatever your faith or personal beliefs, are two of our society's treasured values today. Young people, along with adults, have to make choices about how they will live. This is especially confusing for 11–14s, who already need to make choices as they think about their identity.

Multi-faith, multi-culture

In one middle school we know, there's a prayer room – it's set aside for Muslim students. On Saturday mornings others from the school go to the local temple (they're Hindu), and after school they're learning Gujarati, their grandparents' first language. There's also a school Christian group. There are other faith groups too, all respected and valued. Pupils in this school take for granted their multi-faith world.

Have a look at the facts and figures on the opposite page, taken from the 2001 Census. Whatever your own ethnic roots, culture and everyday experience, today's 11–14s live in a multi-faith, multi-cultural world; at school they sit alongside, are friends with and play sport with people whose skin colour is different, who have different faith backgrounds and who know cultures different from theirs.

This can be incredibly enriching – different beliefs, different customs, different foods, different family structures, a different view of the world. For some, sadly, issues of racism arise, but young people who have friends from different races and cultures aren't likely to be the ones doing the bullying and name-calling.

State schools in Britain actively encourage respect of differences, different faiths and cultures. For some young people from Christian families, our society's cultural and religious diversity can make it easier to go public about your faith. One person is a Muslim; his friend is a Christian. It's an accepted part of who you are. Equally, the Education Act expects state schools to deliver assemblies which are mainly Christian in character. This all raises some big questions for young people trying to work out questions of faith – and identity – for themselves. How do you know that what you believe, or have been taught to believe, is true?

Multi-ethnic...

- Britain's total population is around 59 million.

- The white population is just over 54 million.

- The size of the minority ethnic population was 4.6 million in 2001 – 7.9% of the total population of the United Kingdom.

- Indians are the largest minority group, followed by Pakistanis, those of Mixed ethnic backgrounds, Black Caribbeans, Black Africans and Bangladeshis.

- In Great Britain, the minority ethnic population grew by 53% in the decade between 1991 and 2001, from 3.0 million in 1991 to 4.6 million in 2001.

- Half of the total minority ethnic population were Asians of Indian, Pakistani, Bangladeshi or other Asian origin. A quarter of minority ethnic people described themselves as Black, that is Black Caribbean, Black African or Other Black. Fifteen per cent of the minority ethnic population described their ethnic group as Mixed. About a third of this group were from White and Black Caribbean backgrounds.

Source: Census, April 2001, The UK population: by ethnic group, Office for National Statistics

Multi-faith...

- Nearly 75% of the UK population claim to have a religion.

- Around 72% of the UK population say that their religion is Christian.

- Nearly 3% of the UK population describe their religion as Muslim (1.6 million).

The next largest religious groups:

- Hindus – 559,000

- Sikhs – 336,000

- Jews – 267,000

- Buddhists – 152,000

- Other religions – 179,000

- 16% of the UK population stated that they had no religion (agnostic, atheist, heathens – and 'Jedi Knight').

Source: Census, April 2001, The UK population: by religion, Office for National Statistics

Which truth?

The events of 11 September 2001 in New York raised questions for everyone about truth, right and wrong. The terrorists believed that what they were doing was right and were confident they would be rewarded with paradise. It's an extreme example. But how can 11–14s know, in a plural world, that what we (Christian adults) have taught them to believe is true? 'How do I know it's true?' is a big question which confronts 11–14s as they grow up – and as faith moves from head to heart.

Every day, 11–14s are meeting with people who don't believe what Christians say about God, Jesus, the Bible etc. Respect may be encouraged, but faith is about subjective personal belief, rather than objective truth. At school, a teacher might ask, 'So what do you believe as a Christian? Now, let's hear from someone with different beliefs…' Sooner or later, the young person brought up in church will start asking questions about the 'truth' they've been hearing from adult Christians.

First experiences of 'relativism' can bring uncertainty. It's a characteristic of our time, and 11–14s need lots of opportunities with older Christians to voice some of their questions and doubts. They need support in thinking through the issues, and strategies for speaking about their faith with non-Christians.

Living alongside others who have different beliefs and values doesn't mean 'anything goes'. The good news about Jesus took root in a plural society too. For young Christians today, living in a world which celebrates and affirms difference, the challenge is to have faith, know what you believe and then live it out with humility and respect for others.

What's right? What's wrong?

Imagine Sarah. She is intelligent, likeable, fun-loving, attractive, growing up – and a Christian. At least, she made a commitment to Christ when she was 8 years old and has always, so far, had parents or other Christian adults close by, guiding her. Living as a Christian has been, mainly, straightforward.

Now aged 13, she is starting to have a more independent social life. Her friends are not the kind of people who are likely to commit serious crime, be rude to other people or unkind to animals. But the questions of right and wrong are subtle ones. Without parents around, Sarah has to make decisions. Consider these situations. Similar ones will be familiar for many 11 to 14-year-olds you know.

Sarah's friends swear and use God's name as a swear-word too. When she's with non-Christian friends will she blend and join in? It's easy to do when you hear it all the time. Or will she stand out as different, possibly appearing to judge others? Why shouldn't you swear anyway? Everyone does.

Do you know enough about the main beliefs of other faiths? Do any of the following pieces of information surprise or challenge you?

Muslims believe...

- There is one God, Allah.

- Jesus was a prophet and a great teacher, but not God's one and only Son.

- Muslims accept lots of the Old Testament Scriptures (eg Abraham).

- The holy book of Islam is called the Qur'an and the book itself is treated as special, not just the words.

- As well as some of the Old Testament accounts, the Qur'an contains many detailed rules and regulations.

- Muhammad is the special and holy prophet for Muslims.

- Muslims have five prayer times a day.

- A mosque is the place where Muslims gather to worship.

- Some Muslim women wear the hajib – a head covering – believing that this is following a teaching of their faith about modesty.

- Committed Muslims believe that they should live to please Allah.

- An Imam is the leader of a worshipping community.

- Ramadan is a major annual festival, a month of fasting – showing your commitment to God.

Hindus believe...

- 'Hinduism' is a collection of religions, rather than one belief system.

- Hindus worship many different 'gods', who represent different functions of one supreme deity.

- Hindus follow the direction of a 'guru' – the religious teacher followed by one group.

- The most important Hindu scriptures are the Vedas and the Bhagavad-Gita. The Upanishads are important writings explaining the teachings of the Vedas.

- Diwali – the festival of lights – is the biggest Hindu festival of the year, celebrating the triumph of good over evil, light over dark. It's a time of renewed hope and friendship.

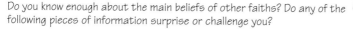

Chapter Link

More about witness in Chapter Seven.

Imagine Sarah...

- Sarah's mum drops her off at the cinema, where she's meeting up with a group of friends. She has told her mum they are going to see a particular film with a 12-certificate. When the group gets to buying tickets, they find that their chosen film is 'full'.

  The group decides to go to another film instead. Only problem: it's a 15-certificate. Some of her friends could pass for 15 and they reckon that in a group, they'll have no problem getting in. Sarah is the only person who's not happy about this. Her mum's gone home. Wouldn't the easiest solution – and least selfish – be to lie about her age and go along with the crowd?

- Sarah's been invited to a sleepover. She thought it was girls only and that one of her friends' parents would be there all the time. When she arrives, she finds that her friend's parents have gone away for the weekend. Some of the boys from her class and her friend's older brother and mates are there too. Someone has brought a bottle of vodka, which is being passed round. Some of the group decide to go out to the local video shop and choose an 18-rated video. Later Sarah realises that nothing has been arranged for where they'll sleep. There's at least one double bed. She notices that one of her best friends is getting very involved with one of the boys from their class. It's too late to phone home now. What should Sarah do? What makes any of this right or wrong anyway?

Deciding about right and wrong...

Experts on ethics and theologians suggest that there are three main approaches to making decisions about what is right or wrong.

- Consequences. Judgement about whether an action is right or wrong is based on whether you think the consequences will be mainly good or bad. Or, you might think about your aimed-for goal and what actions are needed to achieve that.

- Rules. This might seem like the easiest system for making decisions about right and wrong. As long as you follow the rules, whether the results are good or hurtful for others, you've done what's right. Examples include: The Ten Commandments; the teaching of the Qur'an; the laws of your country. There are problems though, for example: Do all the laws of the Old Testament apply today? Is it ever right to break a law (if a special need arises)? What if one person's insistence on keeping a law hurts someone else? And, won't people 'interpret' the rules in different ways?

- Honouring 'virtues'. Here, shared values rather than specific rules, are the benchmark for behaviour and making decisions about right and wrong. For Christians, it involves thinking about what God is like and the teaching of the Bible, then living accordingly, for example: Christians 'virtues' would include loving your neighbour, acting with kindness, forgiving wrongdoing, Different communities and groups 'honour' different 'virtues'.

Get it right – help from the Bible

'Love the Lord your God with all your heart, soul, strength, and mind … Love your neighbours as much as you love yourself.' Jesus said… (Luke 10:27,28)

The Ten Commandments

1   Do not worship any god except me.
2   Don't bow down and worship idols.
3   Do not misuse my name.
4   Remember that the Sabbath Day belongs to me.
5   Respect your father and your mother.
6   Do not murder.
7   Be faithful in marriage.
8   Do not steal.
9   Do not tell lies about others.
10 Do not want to take anything that belongs to someone else.
(See Exodus 20:1–17)

More Bible bits…

Proverbs 3:6   Romans 13:8
Micah 6:8   Galatians 5:22,23
Romans 8:6   John 13:34

Talk/think about…

- How might each of the three approaches on the opposite page help in deciding what's right and what's wrong in the situations facing Sarah (page 42)? You could think up other situations that are about relevant issues for your group too.

- How does each of those three approaches fit with the Bible? Is there a difference between the Old and New Testaments?

- How does a relationship with God help in decision-making?

- Take a look at the Bible references above and at the end of this chapter. How could these help your young people in deciding how to live in today's world?

- What guides your own church community in making decisions about what's right or wrong?

'How do I know what is right or wrong?' is one of the big questions which confronts young Christians as they step out into independence. The problem is that perfectly nice, law-abiding people seem to have different views about what is right or wrong.

It can be a relief for young Christians to realise that there is help and guidance for living in the Bible – and to see that it is a basis for living which 'works' for Christian adults they know. The more knowledge they have of the Bible and the more we can help them develop the skills they need to interpret it and apply it to their lives today, the more they will be able to make their own independent decisions about right and wrong – not just because they want to please parents or other Christian adults, but because they want to please God.

Sexuality

The area of sexuality in today's world is one where it's especially difficult for early adolescents to make God-pleasing decisions. When your body is changing and you're encountering powerful new feelings, it can be difficult to sort out what you think about it all – and that's without the pressures from mates and TV.

PSHE lessons at school will have ensured they know the biological facts and all about contraception. By the time they are 15, they will have got the message from school, mates, TV, their favourite radio station, teen magazines, and the people they live amongst that having sex is OK, as long as: you are 16 (it's legal then), you take precautions so that you don't get pregnant or catch a disease, you respect your partner and that it is a mutual decision. For many young people today, having sex with someone, as long as you're 16, is not at all 'wrong'; it is simply the natural development of a relationship.

Whatever your own church's teaching about the place of sex in human relationships, it's important to recognise that our society is constantly giving 11–14s messages about sex – both heterosexual and homosexual – visually and verbally. A 'loud' silence on the subject from church is not going to help them.

At a stage when they are searching for 'identity' in many aspects of their lives, it may be helpful to encourage them to think about sexuality in terms of 'behaviour' ('Is the way I'm behaving pleasing God?'), rather than 'identity' (which suggests once found, it's fixed).

So for the young person who might be wondering, 'Am I gay?', or the 12-year-old who's troubled by 'going too far', use the Bible to help them think about how God wants them to live and to show them that whatever they have done, God loves them and offers them forgiveness, and will help them live for him. We need to help 11–14s choose to behave in ways which please God, and to discover their identity, in every respect, in Christ.

Peer pressure?

What shapes the values of 11–14s? Here are some findings from two different research projects.

- Family is the most important source of values for this age group. Friends are also important in shaping their values.

- For those who went to church, church was a strong influence on values.

- Teachers are listed well behind family, friends and church as a source of values.

- The young people said that the media itself doesn't influence their values, but they judge what they see and hear via the media by the values they have learned elsewhere.

- The RAKES survey (see *Reaching and Keeping Tweenagers*) found that going to church regularly makes a major impact on values of young people.

- The greatest changes in values take place around the ages of 11 and 12.

Source: Peter Brierley, *Reaching and Keeping Tweenagers*, Christian Research, 2002

The Values Debate

- Worries included: getting AIDS, relationships with others and how attractive they are to the opposite sex.

- They want someone to turn to for advice. Close friends are the most popular source of support, but relationships with parents are very important too.

- Around the same number believed in God as ghosts.

- They're cynical about politics.

- They're not racist.

- Special social concerns are: the environment, Third World poverty and the risk of nuclear war.

- Most don't think it wrong to have sex outside of marriage or under-age.

- Most thought using heroin or sniffing glue is wrong, but that it's OK to get drunk.

- They are law-abiding in issues they feel matter, but are less likely to keep laws that deny them personal freedom, eg restrictions on buying alcohol.

Source: Leslie Francis, *The Values Debate*

Pastorally, 11–14s need support, not coyness. Our society mostly says: 'If it's good for you, do it.' Christians believe, and 11–14s need to know, that there is 'right' and 'wrong', it's OK to say 'No', guilt and forgiveness are God's good gifts to human beings, and they can find a guide for thinking about sexual behaviour in the Bible and within their church community. With other Christians, they need help to explore what the Bible teaches, feel free to ask questions without judgement, and be given the support to live by God's standards. Doing that in today's world can be a daunting challenge. They'll need courage and your prayers.

Life with others

Youth culture

One of the exciting things about moving into the teenage years – apart from starting at secondary school, noticing the first time a boy's head turns as you walked by, or having increasing social independence – is that society now gives you new special status and identity. You are 'youth'. In Chapter Two, we talked about youth culture from the point of view of internal development. In this section, we're thinking about 'youth culture' as an external factor which shapes the lives of 11–14s.

The concept of 'teenagers', meaning the social grouping between childhood and adulthood, began in the middle of the last century. By the 1970s, sociologists recognised that there wasn't just one youth culture with shared tastes in music and dress etc, but many sub-cultures, dependent on various factors (eg social class, economics, education). (See Pete Ward's book *Youth Culture and the Gospel*[1] for more about this.)

'Youth culture' can provide an easy solution for the identity problem. Inclusion in a particular group provides identity and affirmation of who you are. Youth culture's emphasis on peer friendships provides an important source of support for young adolescents during this time of change – especially important today where there's so much uncertainty (eg as a result of divorce).

There are negative implications too: not being included in a group, for example, at school, can mean great loneliness for some young people. Youth culture can also tend to focus attention on problems of young people: emotional, behavioural, social, psychological etc. In fact, most of the 11–14s you know are probably helpful, charming, well-adjusted, kind, thoughtful, responsible and well-behaved. They probably have their 'moments' too, like the adults working with them!

'Youth culture' can also create unhelpful distance between adults and young people at a time when the support of adults is needed. Possibly, this is a reaction against adults excluding them from a world in which they are, in many ways, ready to take part. With the current decline in young people's organisations, there are fewer opportunities for young people and adults to meet. Yet, whilst relationships with adults are changing, they are still needed – to explain, to inform and, as 'someone to lean on'[2]. Relationships with peers and adults are important as young people grow up.

What do 11–14s like doing?

- They like doing things in groups. Hanging out with friends is a top leisure activity. A change for this age group is that now they want to do leisure activities with friends, not with parents or other adult relatives.
- They like being able to choose, not 'told' what to do by adults.
- Favourite activities include: TV watching, listening to music, doing homework, watching DVDs/videos, going to the cinema, computer activities.
- They have a huge range of hobbies and interests. Top ones include: sport, music and dancing.
- Peer group activities are important: they like playing sport, watching TV and videos/DVDs, going to church youth group activities as a group.
- Top solitary activities: computer games and TV.
- Bottom of the list for 11-year-olds is hanging out with a boy or girlfriend.
- Two-thirds of young people questioned for the RAKES survey said they attended an activity in a church hall.

Source: Peter Brierley, *Reaching and Keeping Tweenagers*

Think/talk about…

If peer friendships are a priority for 11–14s, brainstorm different ways of building a group for discipling this age group.

What sort of activities could you include in your programme — both to build friendships, and to use as ways of learning more about faith and growing relationship with God?

If a majority of this age group are happy to go to church buildings for social activities, what ideas does this spark for how 11–14s local to you could be drawn into belief and faith activities within a community of believers?

In the church, 'youth culture' has led to an emphasis on youth work. This is good – but if it means that young people are always apart from the adult congregation, it can cause problems for later. Without the supportive friendships of a youth group, the young adult could later on find themselves isolated, finding they have no independent faith or sense of ease in a mixed-age congregation[3]. How are we helping our group to feel part of the adult congregation, and nurturing an independent relationship with Christ?

'Youth culture' is one of the big 'stories' which shapes the lives of 11–14s, and it permeates another context in which they live and that plays a major part in their formation – school.

School

This is where 11–14s spend most of their waking lives – 39 weeks of the year in fact! – so it has huge impact in shaping their lives. Every weekday they follow a routine which they share with others from quite different backgrounds, social situations, value systems and faiths. The uniting factors are their age and their shared experience of a particular school. Just as they arrive at the point of dramatic changes in their personal physical, psychological and cognitive development, so the move to secondary school brings huge social changes and change in adults' expectations of them in response to their growing maturity.

The 11–14s in your group at church spend most of their days living in this very different world. Mostly, it won't be a Christian context. Superficially, it might look like one culture – school. But on the inside, as with 'youth culture', there is a huge range of different sub-cultures. Moving up to secondary school brings another level in the challenge to discover where you fit, what choices you are going to make – friends, values, behaviour, attitudes – who you are going to become.

Probably, for 11–14s themselves, the most important things about school are the social aspects. These can, of course, be very positive, or very damaging. Friends made in the first few days of secondary school may stay as an important influential group until they leave.

Friendship groups will be formed around shared attitudes to work and authority, levels of ability, extra-curricular interests and activities, everyday tastes in fashion, TV programmes, music etc. Once established as part of that group, where peer-pleasing is more important than adult-pleasing, the young person from a Christian background will be faced every day with a whole range of choices about behaviours and values.

Check out Dan's experience of school.

- Like most young people in England, Wales and Northern Ireland, 11-year-old Dan has just moved from primary to secondary school having just completed Key Stage 2 tests, which will have given the young people some impression of how they are valued and will affect how they see themselves. In Scotland the transition happens at age 12.

- Choice of secondary school was a major issue for Dan and his parents. The school you go to can play a major part in your sense of identity, self-worth and belief.

- Secondary schools are big. There are many teachers and ancillary staff at his new school and loads of buildings, some of which are open to the public too. Dan used to be well-known by all the teachers and pupils at his small primary school. Now, the size of Dan's school makes relationships and the sense of feeling valued difficult – and it's easy to get lost!

- Some of the older students in Dan's school almost seem like adults to him. The older boys are very big and seem quite frightening.

- Now there's even more emphasis on performance and homework. From now until the end of Year 9 is Key Stage 3 and there's lots of pressure to work towards Key Stage 3 tests. Already Dan's parents and his tutor keep reminding them that performance at Key Stage 3 will influence his choice of subjects pursued later. In some schools, it's easy to feel you're not worth much if you are not good at academic subjects.

  - All teaching now happens in specialist subject groups by specialist teachers. Towards the end of Year 9 (third years) when he's aged 14 Dan will have to make choices about subjects for GCSE examinations. The necessity of making choices brings more self-understanding of personal strengths and preferences.

  - With the size of the school community, and everyone wanting to show their independence from adults, teachers seem more distant. Dan is annoyed by some students who are always messing about in lessons. Whilst schools vary in style, most will encourage mutual respect as a basis for living together: respect for students; respect for teachers.

(continued on page 51)

However, some 11–14s don't easily find friends. They may be individualists, natural loners, or might be lacking in self-confidence. If they have problems in discovering where they 'fit', school might be a particularly difficult experience because of bullying, loneliness or just not feeling valued (by fellow students or teachers).

As adults working with 11–14s we need to stay aware of the huge influence that school has on individuals: their happiness, identity and self-worth. In the group you meet at church once a week, a whole range of different experiences of everyday life will be represented. Some will love school, have loads of friends, know they are recognised as being able in particular areas; some will be feeling under great pressure to succeed academically; others will be spending lonely days at school with no friends, feeling that they are not good at anything. In the group at church, they may also feel vulnerable because the more successful members in the group know what they are like at school. Remember, school is a big part of every one of your 11 to 14-year-olds' lives, even though you might not see it.

Home and family: the impact of divorce

Home and family have a big impact on the kind of person 11–14s are, and are becoming. It is one of the most important contexts of their lives for forming values, how they see themselves, other people and the world, and for how their spiritual lives develop. It is parents and grandparents who can do most to help 11–14s embrace Christian faith as their way of living. However, today, the nature of home and family is often uncertain and this can have an impact on 11–14s.

Christians, of course, aren't immune to marriage breakdown: research suggests that children in Christian families experience divorce at half the rate of the wider population[4], which means that some members of your 11–14s group are likely to have experienced their mum and dad separating and the resulting changes in family relationships.

The statistics have particular relevance for those working with 11–14s in church. Whilst this age group are exploring distancing themselves from parental authority in the search for independence, we've seen that stable relationships with family are still needed as sources of advice and support. The separation of parents can disrupt the young person's search for answers to the 'Who am I?' questions.

For many young people, it may also disrupt their regular participation in Sunday services and weekend youth group activities, as they spend time with the 'other' parent. This means there is also a potential disruption to their sense of belonging to a local church and the nurture of their faith – so we'll want to be aware of that and look for ways around it.

Experiencing divorce and family break-up is likely to have other negative results for 11–14s too: at school, in faith matters and in their own attitudes to relationships.

(continued from page 49)

- Dan is now expected to take much more responsibility for his own daily routine, for example: travel to and from school; moving between lessons in school; the planning and organising of his own work.

- Loads of extra-curricular activities bring opportunities for discovering and developing interests and skills and building strong relationships. Dan's really good at football and is picked for one of the school teams. Unfortunately this sometimes means missing midweek or Sunday church activities when training sessions and matches conflict with church activities.

Remember…

School is a huge part of life for 11–14s.

Their friends, activities, the subjects they're good at are part of who they are.

They may be on their own as a Christian. Being different isn't easy, especially when you're 13.

Christian groups in school can be great ways of finding support – and of 'inserting' the gospel into a non-Christian, adult-free zone.

Most young people like school – but for some, it's a very difficult place to be.

Pray for them. How much do you know about their life at school (what they enjoy/find difficult; what they're good at; extras they're involved with; what friends they have; what it's like being a Christian in their school)? Get others in your church praying for them too. In some local areas, Christians get together regularly to pray for their local schools. If there isn't a group in your area, could you start one?

You could give each 11 and 12-year-old in your group a copy of It's Your Move!, a booklet written especially for young people about to start Secondary School. Multi-packs are available at www.scriptureunion.org.uk

Schools Ministry Network www.schoolsministrynetwork.co.uk

51

In the midst of this uncertainty, stable relationships are very important. Friends of the same age can provide advice and emotional support – some of them will have gone through similar experiences – but good relationships with caring adults are essential too. Research shows that for some young people grandparents can also become very important as confidantes for young people of divorcing parents.

How can we offer support to those who are experiencing the consequences of parental separation and divorce? If it's Dad who has left the family, then they may need help in working out how they think about God as Father. Sensitivity will also be needed as we talk about and help them explore God's ideals for marriage and family. Similarly, does our conversation and teaching with the group always assumes a stable two-parent family plus 2.4 children? If so, then some of the group are likely to feel excluded. For the church, the challenge is to provide not just great programmes, but to be a loving community in which young people can be supported by stable, caring and committed relationships with other young people and adults.

Life now

Our multi-faith society, and the influences of people they live alongside (friends, family and school), are all factors which shape the lives of 11–14s. There are some other important features of life in the wealthy West which also shape the lives of 11–14s today.

Consumer story

Shopping is a big leisure pursuit today and is especially significant for 11–14s. It's a relatively safe and enjoyable way for a group of friends to go out together. They can be independent and enjoy being with friends – without adults!

However, the consumer story has bigger significance than just a Saturday afternoon at the shops. Trying on clothes, for all of us, and especially for this age group, is often about trying identities on for size and constructing your chosen image. What do you want to communicate about yourself? It's also, as Graham Cray[5] suggests below, about self-worth.

> 'I am what I consume and what I have.'[6]
> 'Possessions in the form of consumer goods…are related to both self-esteem and well-being.'[7]

How do you value yourself? How do you think others value you? Beyond the shops, 'consumerist' attitudes have permeated all aspects of our society: the media's news and ideas presentation, our relationships, our values, our beliefs.

Alongside the natural exploration of self, there are particular dangers in the 'consumer story' for young people:

11 to 14s' new awareness of freedom, the longing for independence and desire to try on different identities, make the choices presented in the shops (via magazines and TV too) irresistibly tempting. Big business is well aware of the developmental aspirations of this age group and exploits it for profit.

Divorce and its impact…

- Research shows that two in five marriages fail and that by the age of 16, one in four children is likely to have experienced parental divorce.

- Christians divorce at about half the rate of non-Christians.

- The number of divorces is currently fairly static partly because co-habitation without marriage is an increasing trend.

- Young people who are the children of separated and divorced parents are most likely to talk to friends and grandparents about their questions and concerns.

- Divorce and separation of parents…

  …often have negative effects on their children's attitudes to:

  school, sexual morals, drugs, anti-social behaviour, social concerns, religious belief

  …will make it more likely that their children will:

  divorce if they marry, have fewer qualifications, have low status employment

  …and have negative effects on their children's:

  satisfaction with life, sense of purpose, happiness

Research data used in this section on home and family can be found in: Leslie Francis, *The Values Debate*; Peter Brierley, *Steps to the Future*; Peter Brierley, *Reaching and Keeping Tweenagers*

Thinking about divorce…

- What do you believe the Bible teaches about God's view on marriage, faithfulness and divorce?

- How would you respond to the questions of 11–14s whose parents, or friends' parents, are separated or divorced – and support them?

- Brainstorm practical ways in which you could help single-parent families in your church. For example: help with transport needs when these conflict with lone parent's work responsibilities; offer help with things which the lone parent finds difficult (eg chemistry homework, fixing the computer).

More consumer 'dangers'…

- For Christian young people, the temptation is to value themselves and other people according to what they can afford to buy – with the danger that people are devalued and turned into commodities themselves.
- Choices of style can mean exclusion of some people from your group, and, for others, certain material possessions can mean inclusion in the desired group.
- Teenagers today have more material wealth than in any other generation, yet some can't afford to take part in this way of showing their 'worth'.
- The 'consumer story' places emphasis on 'now', not valuing your history or hopes and dreams for tomorrow. Consequently, it's an uncertain world and one where disappointment is inevitable: what you buy today is out of fashion tomorrow.
- The emphasis on immediate gratification means that ideas of waiting, patience and perseverance, whether in material or spiritual terms, are devalued.
- Whilst it feels as though there is freedom and choice, it's really about control (eg what you look like, what music you listen to, what leisure pursuits you are into). Often this control is exercised by external (and not particularly impartial!) factors.

All this presents some contrasts with what God wants for his people: the valuing of individuals for who they are; a bias towards valuing the poor; allowing your life to be shaped by God's. It also poses questions about the approaches and styles we use to communicate Christian truths to young people.

Magazines

- More likely to be read than books – although *Harry Potter, Lord of the Rings*, and, for younger girls, books by Jacqueline Wilson, have bucked the trend – magazines are quick to read and can be read in a piecemeal kind of way. Like shopping, they have a social function, providing ideas to share with others; they are about image too and discovering more about who you are through trying on different identities. Magazines are also about 'now'. If you still have any of your own teen mags from your youth, try showing these to 11–14s you know – and wait for their reaction!
- Magazines for girls aged 10+, perhaps more than shopping, subtly (and in some cases, not so subtly) provide a moral code for living. Just take a look along the teen section of magazines (*Shout, Bliss, Cosmo Girl*) at your local supermarket and spot the messages from the front covers about: image, relationships, values. Problem pages have a major focus on issues such as: 'going out', loneliness and self-harm.
- Boys who are not into the pop and TV magazines, are most likely to be reading interest magazines (eg *Shoot, Nintendo*) which, whilst they can be intensely individualistic, can also have a positive social function, providing a focus for conversation.

Like magazines, television can be socially uniting too, as young people talk today about last night's TV programmes (eg *The Simpsons, Neighbours,* the big football match).

1 Read Matthew 6:24–34.

2 Think/talk about…

- What are 11–14s worried about?
- What things are important to the 11–14s you know?
- How can God help them with the things that bother them?
- How can you help them care more about God than money, clothes and possessions?

Find out more…

If you're interested in how big business is exploiting young people here are two more books to get you thinking…

A. Quart, *Branded: The Buying and Selling of Teenagers*, Arrow, 2003

N Klein, *No Logo*, Flamingo, 2000

'If you own this child at an early age, you can own this child for years to come …' Gary Ruskin[5].

Television

Teenagers are, of course, massively exposed to the influence of television and the big picture it gives of life and how it should be lived. There is hardly a single teenager in Britain who doesn't live with a television, many having TV in their own bedrooms.

- It's a visual world. Opinions are presented as facts, and reality is reduced to sound-bites. Like other parts of life today, it's about choosing. You switch on and choose what you like. It's one more 'mirror' where 11–14s are looking for their reflection.
- In TV-land, all truth is 'relative' and messages about a moral framework for living are confusing. For example, a popular soap like *Neighbours* has positive and appealing themes about friendship, but often reinforces values which don't fit with a biblical view of one-to-one relationships.
- TV adverts and focus on celebrity all communicate powerful messages about image, wealth, worth, how to live – and how to be happy.
- Positive consequences of television include: awareness of how others live and of the wealth of the West and poverty in other places; discussion and information about important issues; it's a good resource for enjoyment and shared experiences. It also gives young people a common 'language' for talking about life and meaning.

TV is part of our world, and is very important for 11–14s – but watching TV can take a lot of 11–14s' time. Think about the potential for that time being spent in other ways. For example, apart from homework and other responsibilities, what about the time which could be given instead to reading the Bible, praying, or at a church group?

However, in spite of high viewing figures, recent research suggests that young teenagers aren't watching as much TV as they once were. Perhaps this is due to the other small screen.

Computers and electronic communications

For many young teenagers the interactive nature of electronic media is now more appealing than TV. Nearly all 11–14s in this country will have access to a computer and the web, if not at home, then at school. But most, probably especially those likely to be part of your church group, will have a computer at home, and, like TV, many will have one in their bedroom.

- The most common uses of the computer and web are for homework, information, entertainment (games) and communication.
- Like other aspects of contemporary life, computers emphasise the present moment and fragmented living, as different images and ideas come in quick succession.
- The intensely individualistic and physically passive nature of computer activities causes concern. On the other hand, they (and game systems, like GameCube) can be strongly 'social', for example: as friends look at a TV screen together; as common interests for conversation; as a means of information exchange and relationship with unseen others through interest websites across the world.

Drugs and alcohol

Are drugs and alcohol part of the world of 11–14s who go to church? The following is a part of a conversation with two young Christians (names disguised).

Do people you know at school take drugs?

Ben: Yeh, 'course.

Is it something loads of people do?

Lucy: No – adults make it seem like everyone's doing drugs, but they're not. Just some people do.

What kind of drugs?

Ben: Cannabis, mainly – just soft stuff.

What about heroin or ecstasy?

Lucy: Don't be stupid. Where would 13-year-olds get it? They couldn't afford it anyway! No, most people who take cannabis just use it sometimes if they can get it.

Ben: The people who take drugs might take ecstasy if they can get it.

What about under-age drinking?

Ben: Yeh, everyone does that!

What do they drink?

Lucy: Cans, Bacardi – anything they can get.

Where do they drink?

Ben: At parties, anywhere…

But not to get drunk?

Lucy: Yes! That's why they drink!

Why?

Lucy: So you can say to your mates next day how drunk you got last night…

Ben: No, it's not that. They think drinking loads will make them feel good.

What research says…[9]

- A survey for *Bliss* magazine found:

  …around 44 per cent of the young people interviewed had been offered drugs.

  …under-age drinking is a big problem. More than six out of ten 15-year-olds had been drunk.

- Research amongst 11 to 15-year-olds by Leslie Francis found that they were:

  …very tolerant about alcohol

  …less tolerant about marijuana

  …intolerant about heroin and solvents.

- Another report found that binge drinking is commonplace amongst young teens, with a quarter of 13 and 14-year-olds claiming to have drunk more than five alcoholic drinks in one session.

More about electronic communications…

- Dangers include the excessively time-consuming nature of computer activity; and the obvious dangers of going to websites that can harm in some way.
- Particular factors to remember when encouraging 11–14s to use the web in connection with your church group's programme include: 11–14s, unlike older young people, often have firmly imposed parental limitations concerning time spent on the computer, purpose of use and websites which they are allowed to visit; the computer's often a household resource in a 'public' space which is shared with others.
- Emails, MSN and texting: 11–14s are intensely relational, and they use the 'new' media for relationships; they check emails every day, multi-task with MSN messaging whilst doing homework on the computer, and text via their mobile anytime, anywhere, through the day. Contrary to fears that electronic communications would be anti-relational, for young people they usually are mainly relational.
- An easy-to-miss characteristic of electronic media is that they are 'owned' by the young people. For young Christians, it's their way of expressing and sharing faith in a space not controlled by adult Christian language and ideas.

The now-not-so-new 'new' media have potential, already being released, for a multitude of new ways of sharing youth group communications, encouragement, prayer, Bible engagement, nurture etc. How big is your imagination?

Music

'There is a constant dialogue between popular music and youth culture.' Pete Ward[10]

For most adolescents, music is the backdrop to their lives. Whereas some adults find it difficult to concentrate on work with music playing, many teenagers find it difficult to concentrate without.

11–14s like many different styles. It's OK not to like Top of the Pops. Softer popular jazz currently seems to have increasing appeal to young teenagers, with younger artists picking up the music of yesteryear. Meanwhile, Goths are still into heavy metal bands. As ever, music which might sound rebellious and which stands out from the crowd helps its followers (who may feel excluded from other mainstream groups) to feel they belong – at the same time giving them power to exclude others.

So, if music is such an important medium for the age group, how are you using it with your group and how can it be used better for helping people learn and grow in faith? There are lots of resources available to help you use lyrics and music to explore faith and life themes with your teenagers.

Take time out to visit a music store near you (eg HMV, Virgin Megastore) and take a look at the top 40 albums and singles. Stand and watch for a bit – notice who's buying what. Talk to the 11–14s you know. Ask them what they like, what their friends like, when and why they listen to music. Do the words matter? You might be surprised. Their criteria for evaluating music may be very different to yours.

TV, computers and Net – facts and figures

- Western teenagers in the 1990s were watching 20-25 hours per week of television. Recent research suggests TV viewing rates are declining.

- However, television-watching is the most popular activity for 11–14s in their spare time.

- Most popular programmes are comedy, films, soaps and cartoons.

- Research suggests that TV doesn't affect attitudes to Christianity.

- Recent research suggested that 81 per cent of 11–14s have access to a computer and the Internet. Some 11–14s have their own computer with Net access in their bedroom. All secondary students in Britain have access to computers and the Net at school.

- Things 11–14s like about the Net are: it's an easy source of information, useful for homework; enjoyable possibilities on offer like games to download and TV programme websites; the communication possibilities to talk with other people.

- Things they don't like: technical difficulties like the time it takes to log on and download; the cost and arguments about who pays; unwanted emails and adverts.

Sources:

Peter Brierley, *Reaching and Keeping Tweenagers*

Leslie Francis and Harry Gibson, 'The influence of age, sex and social class on TV viewing time and programme preferences among 11–15 year olds', in *Journal of Educational Television*, Vol 19, No 1, 1993

Michael Budde, *The (Magic) Kingdom of God: Christianity and Global Culture Industries*, Westview Press, 1997

Don Tapscott, *Growing Up Digital*

Formation or transformation?

There is not space to include here all the factors in today's world which are shaping the lives of 11–14s – and these will vary according to 11–14s' choices and situation. But there are common themes: deciding who you want to be, the value we place on ourselves and other people, emphasis on the immediate, emphasis on choice.

It's easy to end up with a fairly negative picture of what all this means for young people who are learning about following Jesus in today's world. However, there are some positive opportunities in all this…

- Christianity was born into a 'plural' world. The early disciples had to make a choice to follow Jesus. The need to make a choice – rather than just being a Christian because of where you grew up – has always meant serious reflection and definite commitment.
- The 'counter story' of Christianity is very different to the consumerism which surrounds everyone in the Western world. Christian 11–14s can make a difference, especially if we support them through modelling God's values ourselves.
- Contemporary communications offer fantastic opportunities for spreading the good news about Jesus and for discipling and nurturing young people in faith.
- Media has great and powerful potential for communicating God's love and welcome to young people, both those in and outside of Christian community.
- Christianity offers the security of acceptance for who you are, valuing of the past and hope for the future. It emphasises imagination against the limits of today's current fashion.
- Surrounded with consumer culture, there are questions for the church about methods and models used to help young people choose to find their identity within the different 'story' of Christian faith.

Materially well-off or not, young people who find their security in Christ and in their Christian community can be transformed by their faith, rather than 'formed' by external factors – and also do some shaping and subverting of society's values themselves, if they decide to live God's way.

Pray for each young person as they cope with the challenges of following Christ in today's world.

Some starting points for getting a biblical viewpoint:

Multi-faith/multi-ethnic: Deuteronomy 5:7; Deuteronomy 10:17–20.

Whose truth?: John 14:1–14; Acts 16:16–34; Colossians 4:2–6.

What's right? What's wrong?: Exodus 20:1–17; Proverbs 3:6; Micah 6:8; Luke 10:27,28; Romans 13:8.

Home and family: Deuteronomy 5:16; Matthew 19:3–11; Colossians 3:18 – 4:1.

Consumer story: Matthew 6:19–21; Matthew 16:25,26; Matthew 19:16–30; Luke 12:13–34; Luke 16:13; James 5:1–6.

Drugs and alcohol: Proverbs 20:1; Ecclesiastes 2:3; Galatians 5:16–24; Ephesians 5:15–21; Deuteronomy 7:12,13; Psalm 104:14,15; John 2:1–11.

Music: Ephesians 5:15–21; Colossians 3:15–17; Psalm 150.

Transformation: Romans 12:1,2; Matthew 5:13–16; Matthew 13:33; Ephesians 4:17 – 5:2.

References for Chapter Three

1   Pete Ward, Youth Culture and the Gospel
2   Paul Fenton, Someone to Lean On
3   Pete Ward, ibid, p60
4   Peter Brierley, Steps to the Future, p56
5   Graham Cray, Postmodern Culture and Youth Discipleship, p8
6   Barrie Gunter and Adrian Furnham, Children as Consumers, p43, quoted by Graham Cray in Postmodern Culture and Youth Discipleship
7   Ibid, p43
8   Quoted in Tom and Christine Sine, Living on Purpose
9   Sources: Sarah Womack, Daily Telegraph, 'Moral Code of the Right Young Things', 11 March, 2004; Peter Brierley, Steps to the Future; Leslie Francis, The Values Debate; Peter Brierley, Reaching and Keeping Tweenagers
10 Pete Ward, ibid, p82

Further reading and resources

Claire Pedrick and Andy Morgan, Under Pressure

Peter Brierley, Reaching and Keeping Tweenagers

Lesslie Newbigin, The Gospel in a Pluralist Society

Leslie Francis, The Values Debate

Don Tapscott, Growing Up Digital

About school…

Scripture Union in Schools, 207-209 Queensway, Bletchley, MK2 2EB
www.scriptureunion.org.uk/schools

re:source – ideas for school groups. Find it at www.scriptureunion.org.uk

Chapter Four – Spiritual Development of 11–14s

A time for growth

Kate had always gone to church with her mum and dad. Her grandparents are Christians too. Bible stories, 'sorry, please and thank you' prayers, Christian songs, Christian events, and in the last couple of years, Scripture Union holidays, have all been enjoyed and accepted as part of normal life. Now aged 11, with secondary school on the horizon next September, Kate is definitely growing up. She seems less happy than she used to be in church. Some of her friends there have left because they've moved. She says she's feeling too old for 'Sunday school' and is bored.

A few months later, Kate's at her new secondary school. She has new friends. They regularly go out together, shopping and to see films. A 'sleepover' at one of her mates' houses raises the question of church the next morning. Her parents could say 'no' to the sleepover and drag their resentful daughter to church the next day. But they reach a compromise and pick up a resigned and tired daughter on the way to church.

Over the next few weeks, it's obvious that Kate feels out of place in the activities on offer for her at her church. She is now definitely a young woman rather than a child, yet the youth group, which does appeal to Kate, is for young people of 14 and up. There aren't many other 12-year-olds in the church – and, alongside her school friends, they just seem too 'Christian'. Adults in her church, apart from her parents, don't really seem to notice her. Not surprisingly, hanging out with her real friends at weekends seems much more appealing. They are nice people, but God doesn't seem to be a significant part of their lives.

Whilst the Christian values at home have been formative, now the values and lifestyles of her non-Christian friends are beginning to shape her life. This influence becomes more powerful just at the moment when it's important for Kate to distance herself from familiar adult authority figures, when she will instinctively begin to question all previously given beliefs, and at a time when she will be looking to peers to affirm her identity.

Choose for yourselves this day whom you will serve … as for me and my household, we will serve the Lord' (Joshua 24:15,NIV)

A time for choosing…

With growing self-awareness, 11–14s begin to make independent choices about most things, including having to decide whether to put God or themselves first.

Talk/think about:

What choices are facing 11–14s you know where their Christian faith could make a difference? For example:

- Going, or not going, to church
- Swearing
- Being unkind to/gossiping about/bullying others
- Lying
- Under-age drinking
- Disobeying parents
- Reading the Bible

How could you (and other Christians) help them make good choices? For example:

- Help them to use the Bible to know how God wants them to live.
- Model God's way of living.
- Talk about the sorts of choices they need to make every day.
- Encourage them to find friends who will support them in their living for God.
- Help them to develop a personal relationship with God.

Making choices about what's the right or wrong thing to do can be a great opportunity for taking one step closer to God. Pray for each of your young people in the choices they are learning to make at the moment – that the decisions they make will bring them closer to God.

Christian parents and church leaders might think that young people like Kate are giving up on Christian faith. But this is probably not the case. They might now feel uncomfortable with the social experience of 'going to church', but that doesn't mean that their Christian beliefs and sense of relationship with God have evaporated. In fact, the time when the young person starts saying they're not sure about going to church any more may signal a significant opportunity for spiritual growth. But it does raise questions for us about how to make 'church' a welcoming place for young people.

Every young person is different, but in this chapter we're going to look at some theories and general principles of spiritual development, which alongside other aspects of 11 to 14-year-olds' development, suggest that, whatever they are like, this time has great potential for growth.

Faith development theories

Choosing your gods

Psychologists have said that the question of how to live your life – or 'choosing your gods'[1] – is a central one for adolescence. Some theologians give a different picture of how Christians are learning to live their lives, with the idea of believers being part of an ongoing story (the biblical story) which they 'indwell' or inhabit[2].

Adolescents, whether or not they've been brought up in Christian families, are looking for 'gods' and a 'story' to indwell – a place where they feel they belong, a 'story' which makes sense of their world, and in which they have a role. The adolescent's growing drive to discover meaning and purpose in life brings a desire for commitment. Working with young people, you will know that such 'commitments' might be a transient enthusiasm, or the beginning of a life-time given to a cause, for example, environmentalism – or to the Christian faith. Either way, this stage of life has great potential for a response to commitment to Christ as Lord of their lives.

Spirituality, religion and faith

Theologian John Hull has written helpfully about the difference between spirituality, religion and faith[3], giving a picture of three concentric circles: the outer is spirituality, the next is religion, at the centre is faith.

He argues that all human beings are essentially spiritual beings – having an inborn desire for something bigger than just the material world. However, in his view, spirituality does not necessarily include religion – meaning shared beliefs, and where individuals see themselves in relation to and under God. Faith's a further category within the religious, which John Hull defines as a 'trustful response to the object of religious worship'[4]. This model suggests that even though someone thinks of themselves as a member of a particular religion, they may not necessarily have faith themselves.

The 'churched' 11–14s we're thinking about in this book are already in the 'religious' circle, but, for many, faith has still to be owned as they meet Jesus for themselves and submit to him as Lord. So, how can we help those brought up in the Christian 'religion' grow into independent faith?

Spirituality, religion and faith

Think about the 11 to 14-year-olds that you are working with.

- What signs do you see of their 'spirituality'?

- Why might they think of themselves as members of the Christian religion?

- What signs do you see in individuals of a faith response to God?

- What actions or questions might help the young people in your group move from knowledge about the Christian faith to knowing God for themselves?

Will they, won't they?

Wayne Dixon, now a Scripture Union schools worker, started going to church because it meant he could play in the football team. Wayne recalls:

'I wasn't really interested in the Bible part but got my first introduction to the gospel… And I got to play in the football team.'

One New Year's Eve there was a special social evening at church followed by a watchnight service where the speaker challenged people to start the New Year on God's side. Wayne, aged 11, had already heard about Jesus…

'But until then, it was all history and knowledge. None of it was personal. But here was this speaker saying "What about being on God's side?" and I decided right then, that … If Jesus did all this for me, then I wanted my life to count for him … I wanted to follow him.'

Source: Ken Edgecombe, *Will they or won't they?*, pp55–67

Chapter Link

For more on 11–14s in the life of the church, see Chapter Six and Chapter Nine.

Developing faith

There are several well-known theories about how faith develops. Whilst such theories might not fit our own personal experience of how we, or others who we know, are growing in faith, they can provide useful starting points for thinking about what's happening in our own lives and the lives of the young people we want to disciple.

James Fowler's understanding of faith is not just limited to religious faith, but is more about how all human beings find meaning in their lives, perhaps similar for the adolescent to the identity search already discussed. In his book, *Stages of Faith*, he describes faith in various stages, which can be taken as corresponding with chronological ages as people move through life. John Westerhoff, similarly, has described 'styles' of faith, assumed as Christian faith within a believing community, and usually associated with particular ages[5]. However, these descriptions of faith development are not necessarily to do with age.

The theorists agree that adolescent growth in faith builds on the experience of childhood. This, of course, emphasises the great importance of how we build faith throughout childhood before adolescence. Westerhoff describes the faith of childhood as 'experienced faith' – it's learnt and expressed through experience. However, the onset of adolescence triggers a new stage.

Westerhoff's 'affiliative faith' stage, usually associated with early adolescence, stresses the importance of finding identity in relationships, and assumes, for the purposes of faith development, that these will be within a stable church community (often not easy to achieve in contemporary Britain). Reflecting the broader developmental picture, Francis Bridger[6] draws out three characteristics of 'affiliative faith': the herd instinct, meaning young people identify with friends' opinions, rather than finding individual faith; the dominance of feelings, rather than intellectual integrity; and the questioning of authority. All of these, you will probably recognise as you think about your 11–14s group. All have practical implications for the ways in which we help 11–14s grow in faith.

Whilst James Fowler's 'conforming faith' and Westerhoff 's 'affiliative faith' are usually linked with early adolescence, neither are rigidly connected with age group, and, today, with the increasingly early onset of adolescence, some young teenagers seem to be moving into Fowler's and Westerhoff's later stages – 'choosing faith' and 'searching faith' where conforming to the group becomes less important than working out for yourself what you believe.

One way of seeing faith develop...

John Westerhoff's model for faith development relates to people who are brought up through church. His 'styles' of faith are often loosely connected to different stages of development. Here's a summary of his faith 'styles':

Experienced faith (childhood)

Faith is learnt as it is expressed through trusting relationships. Experience and knowledge of faith is stored up for later developments.

Affiliative faith (early adolescence)

As the young person grows up they need to feel they belong to a Christian community. Their faith is strengthened as they are allowed to participate, and have responsibility, in the activities of church. A strong sense of belonging also helps young Christians to learn and identify with their community's Christian 'story'.

Searching faith (later adolescence)

Some young people then move into searching faith. Having experienced and learnt the 'story', they have doubts and questions as they compare what they know with other understandings of life. It's an important stage for preparation for personally owned faith. Sadly, it's a stage when many young people choose not to 'go to church' any more.

Owned faith (young adulthood)

Owned faith is when there is a major change in the person's behaviour – their thinking, feeling, and willing. Their whole life takes on a new direction as they discover their personal identity in relationship with God. Now, the believer will want to stand up for what they believe and witness in their words and actions.

Source: John H Westerhoff III, *Will Our Children Have Faith?*

Doubts and questions

Doubts, uncertainty and questioning are a natural part of the wider developmental process for adolescents. The questioning process is driven by the desire to find out what you 'believe' and to decide how you want to live your life: 11–14s will instinctively want to find their own answers to the big questions of life and faith. In Westerhoff's 'searching faith' stage, questioning and desire for commitment hone each other. And in the Bible we see that questioning often preceded commitment or new understanding of relationship with God (eg Samuel, Jesus, the apostles, the Ethiopian eunuch).

For Westerhoff, this necessary questioning of faith needs to take place within the security of their faith community. Young people need to feel they have permission to ask questions and express doubts and uncertainty. Not to allow this, or to try to force personal commitment to Christian faith, before the individual is ready, is damaging.

So, remember, when 11–14s start to ask questions like…

> 'Did Jesus really rise from the dead?'
> 'How can we know for sure that God exists?'

… this is a moment for praise, not panic! Doubts and uncertainty expressed do not mean the death of faith, rather they signal the young person is wanting to grow in faith as they move towards adulthood. And, if you are on the receiving end of such doubts and questions, be encouraged: the young person doing the questioning feels secure enough in their relationship with you and in your faith in God to express their uncertainties.

Nurture or conversion?

Belonging and believing

What brought you to the point when you knew you were a Christian? What helped you move from simply having a set of beliefs which made sense to you as a basis for living, to your present relationship with and commitment to Jesus as Lord of your life?

For a few Christians reading this, it might have been an amazing moment of revelation, when, having had no previous contact with Christians, you were suddenly aware of God and received him into your life. You believed, then you discovered where you belonged. However, for most reading this, there will be stories of lifelong nurture by family, friends and church – all of which built your awareness of God, his ways and Word. As you were part of the Christian community, so you grew in awareness of his love for you, his call to you. It was this which led to a moment of commitment, or to a gradual realisation that you were a disciple of Jesus, in relationship with him.

FAQs

Their friends don't believe it. Their RE teacher asks them why they believe it. And lots of people believe in different things. In any case, there's the pull of loads of stuff which they'd love to do, but older Christians have given them the impression that it's wrong.

It's not surprising they have doubts, ask questions and want answers. This is one of the most exciting and rewarding things about working with this age group. Sometimes, it's as though these questions have never been asked before and finding the answers is 'life-and-death' important.

Take time to talk about doubts and answer their questions. No matter how familiar to us, our answers might play a crucial part in helping that young person grow in their commitment to God.

What answers might you give to these? Keep them simple!

- How do we know what we believe is 'true'? Maybe other faiths are 'true'?
- If you can be forgiven, whatever you do, why not carry on living as you want anyway?
- What's the point of being a Christian?
- Why should I go to church?
- How do you know the Bible is true?
- If God is a loving God, why does he allow…

  …all the awful things which are happening in our world?

  …my mum and dad to split up?

- I'm not sure Jesus really did rise from the dead.
- God doesn't answer when I pray.
- I'm such a bad person – I don't feel that God will forgive me.
- I don't think God has come into my life – I don't feel close to him.
- I'm not sure I believe in Christianity any more.
- I can't believe a loving God would send people to hell.

The 'traditional' evangelical understanding of conversion has been described as the moment when a person decides to accept Christ into their life[7]. Francis Bridger suggests, however, that a more helpful model might be the idea of 'belonging first, believing second'[8]. In the Bible, as we saw in Chapter One, young people were able to respond to God's direction, because they were already part of a believing community. The apostles grew in their belief and understanding of Jesus as they were part of his special group of friends. Gradually, they came to understand who he was, and after uncertainty, doubt and failure, they chose lifelong commitment, which in turn enabled them to disciple others.

The theories of James Fowler and John Westerhoff suggest that growing in faith towards independent Christian commitment takes place within the nurture of families and communities. Again, belonging leads to believing. So, one way of seeing conversion is as a culmination of a nurturing process over time.

The work of the Holy Spirit

Alongside the theoretical grids which help us think about what is happening, there is the dimension of how God, the Holy Spirit, is at work in the lives of the 11–14s we meet each week. He is even more motivated than we are about all this and wants to bring each one of them to himself – '… only God's Spirit can change you into a child of God' (John 3:6). The work of God's Spirit is also about transformation – little by little we understand more and grow more like Jesus (Romans 12:1,2; Galatians 5:22,23). Whilst this is true for all ages, 11–14s, because of their age and stage of development, may be particularly ready to respond to God's Spirit.

Jesus' talk with Nicodemus made it clear that there is no way into the kingdom of God without the work of the Spirit (John 3:8). So, as we work with 11–14s, we need to cultivate our own awareness that God is already at work in each of their lives. When they ask questions about God and life (like Nicodemus and Jesus), we need to be ready to give challenge and opportunities for commitment – not to pressurise, but to help them move one step closer to God.

So, quietly celebrate every positive response towards God, and look for and encourage signs of that faith worked out in changed attitudes and behaviour. On the other hand, patience and understanding are necessary for the times when they seem to give up on faith. In the end 'conversion' is the Spirit's work and we may not know the moment when that particular step happens.

Biblical models – saying 'Yes' to Jesus

The apostles (The Gospels): From call to commitment, the disciples go through ups and downs of misunderstandings, questions and growing faith leading to understanding.

The disciples on the Emmaus road (Luke 24:13–35): Confusion led to questions, then recognition of Jesus as he walked alongside them.

The Ethiopian Official (Acts 8:26–38): Already studying the Scriptures and asking questions, Philip told him about Jesus, resulting in his commitment to Christ.

Saul (Acts 9:1–18): Revelation on the Damascus road brought immediate life-change.

Cornelius (Acts 10): A desire to live God's way led to a meeting with Peter, who explained the gospel: Cornelius and his family were converted.

Lydia (Acts 16:11–15): She was trying to live for God. Then Paul explained about Jesus: she was converted.

Biblical pictures

The Bible provides us with several helpful analogies for spiritual growth.

- Birth
John 3:1–21: you must be born again.
Titus 3:4–7: the meaning of 'new birth'.
Romans 8:1–17: living by the Spirit.

- Journey
Exodus – Joshua: the journey of God's people to the Promised Land.

- Growth
John 15:1–17: the vine, branches and pruning.
Matthew 13:1–9,18–23: the importance of good ground.
Psalm 1:3: planting by water.
Galatians 5:16–25: the results of good growth.

- Building
1 Peter 2:4,5: living stones being built…

Think/talk about…

Think carefully about the Bible material on this page. Then talk/think about these questions.

- How could you 'create' good conditions for growth (eg help them learn from the Bible, allow questions)?

- How could you help your group grow in faith (eg take time to talk to individuals)?

- What might help the 11–14s you know say 'Yes' to Jesus (eg be ready to ask challenging questions)?

At some point you may notice that an individual has a clear sense of *knowing* God for themself, rather than simply *knowing* facts about him. God alone knows the moment at which this happened and, anyway, the 'process' – nurture and conversion – does not end for us with individual commitment. Christians need to keep growing and being transformed. Young Christians need ongoing support, as do their leaders, if faith is to continue to grow towards their being made perfect in Christ: '… we continue to preach Christ to each person … in order to bring each one into God's presence as a mature person in Christ' (Colossians 1:28, NCV). That's the goal!

Whenever the move from 'religion' to 'faith' happens, whatever God uses to prompt belief from head to heart, the young person's response is likely to be within the context of lengthy, committed nurture in a believing community.

The role of the believing community

The nurture and shaping of Christian faith throughout childhood is enormously significant in preparing the young person to move from dependent to independent faith as they grow into adulthood. The kind of faith-modelling they experience whilst pre-adolescent can have major influence on their later independent-faith commitments.

There are many ways in which adolescents might be experiencing Christian community as well as in their 'local church' where you meet them: Christian family; a Christian holiday; Christian friends at school; a youth group; a web-based group – all have potential to be significant ways of encountering Christ, as love for him and his life are modelled in relationships.

Chapters Six, Seven and Nine all look in more practical detail at the importance of church for nurturing faith in 11–14s and the ways in which Christian community can carry out this ministry. For now, here are some of the key people for helping 11–14s grow in faith:

Parents and family

Christian parents have been teaching and modelling faith to their children throughout their lives – through information given, through words and actions, through teaching about relationship with God in Bible-reading, prayer and worship. Practically, they have transported their children to church activities and events. They have made decisions which mean their children have had opportunities to learn more about faith. Even where parents are not Christian believers, the influence of Christian grandparents can be significant in similar ways (see Peter Brierley, *Reaching and Keeping Tweenagers*, p19 onwards).

As 11–14s put more distance between themselves and parents, Bible-reading and prayer times begin to be left to the young person now, but there are many ways for parents to continue quietly supporting their faith development: lifts to Christian events, encouragement to participate in Christian activities, challenging questions when (and where) appropriate, advice, modelling the faith, obtaining Bible notes for them etc. Part of this 'supporting role' involves trusting others in encouraging and nurturing the faith of your child.

... Christ Jesus himself ... the chief cornerstone. In him the whole building is joined together ... (Ephesians 2:20,21, NIV)

Jesus, the reason why...

11–14s brought up in the church are familiar with teaching about Jesus' death and resurrection, but somehow the importance of recognising sin, the possibility of forgiveness and new life become 'something Christians believe', without really understanding the uncompromising and transforming challenge that Jesus brings to our lives.

Maybe we're wary of loading young people with guilt, preferring to emphasise God's love and acceptance. Yet Jesus' death and resurrection are the cornerstone of our faith. The moment when a 12-year-old realises and is troubled by the fact that they have done something which has let down, not only their parents, but God too, then the power of Jesus has touched their lives and there is an opportunity for genuine response to God.

Recognition of having done wrong, understanding of the possibility of forgiveness and the reassurance that God has not deserted you, but is with you to help you change, is good news. Providing opportunities for such recognition of sin may be significant times, helping 11–14s grow in their knowledge of God and love for Jesus.

Take a look at these Bible/passages verses:

- John 3:16
- Romans 10:9
- 1 Corinthians 15:17

What do you find difficult about helping 11–14s understand the importance of Jesus' life, death and resurrection?

How might you build into your work with them opportunities to help them understand more?

Other adult leaders

These might include: group leaders in your church, leaders at a Christian holiday or event, the adult leader of a school Christian group, a Christian teacher. Whatever the situation, the Christian adult leader's role with young people is to facilitate that young person's relationship with God. At this critical time for faith development, 11–14s need leaders who they can talk to, who they feel appreciate and understand them. They might not feel able to talk to parents about faith and current life issues, but their Christian group leader can provide the opportunities the young person needs for conversation about God – that might also include challenging questions about faith commitment as the leader observes the spiritual growth of the young person.

Older teenagers

… are in touch with the life and experience of 11–14s in a way that adult Christians can't be. And, in today's world, they are choosing to follow Jesus. They can be brilliant role models – with a key role in discipling younger teens, for example: as Christian group leaders; as team members on a Christian holiday; as junior leaders of groups at church; cell group leaders; as one-to-one Christian mentors; and as older friends. They might not have much experience, or knowledge – but from the young teenager's perspective they can be an attractive and compelling reason for faith in Jesus.

Same-age young people

… can provide great support for one another in their growth in faith. Encourage them to pray together for each other: in cell groups at church; in their Christian group and informal friendship networks at school; via texting, email, MSN and interactive website groups. See Chapter Three and Chapter Eight for more on this.

Peer group friendships are a very important part of growing up. They're important for faith growing too. So…

Get a group

- Intensely relational, 11–14s need friendship groups where they feel safe and which they enjoy being part of. If there isn't a Christian group like this for them, they will find another 'group'. If numbers at your church make having a special 11–14s' group impossible, could you suggest churches in your area organise regular or occasional joint events?
- They need opportunity to ask questions of adults and to talk together about what they believe.
- They need to have fun together and space to form genuine relationships so that they can talk about what God means to them.
- Doing social stuff together, frequently emailing and texting each other, reinforces relationships, Christian values and beliefs. The group friendship helps them feel it's OK – and sometimes, great – to be a Christian, and it's OK to be different from the mainstream.
- A lively, friendly group can be a great way of attracting others who haven't had any experience of Christian faith. Belonging might lead to believing, as they discover their identity in Jesus through finding acceptance and their place in the family of God.

Leadership style for working with 11–14s

- … acknowledges the growing maturity of 11–14s.

- … recognises that 11–14s want to be involved in what happens and not be bossed about.

- … understands that 'authoritative' isn't 'authoritarian'.

- In his book, *Someone to Lean On*, Paul Fenton suggests that adult Christians working with young adolescents should think of themselves as 'fellow travellers' – who just happen to have a bit more knowledge and experience.

- Relationship and friendship are important, but 11–14s still need to feel there's an adult who knows where they're heading, knows what to do if things go wrong, and won't let things get out of control.

- Be generous with time, attention and listening to each individual in your group.

- Warning: be careful about appearing to pay more attention to some young people than others. Be aware of the possibility that someone in the group might have a 'crush' on you. Stay alert to your own weaknesses and don't be flattered or enticed by admiring looks. Discourage emotional dependence on you – we're growing disciples of Jesus not ourselves! Avoid hurt by being sensible about noticing the nature of 'deep-and-meaningful' conversations. Ensure you're never alone with a young person in your care.

- Acceptance of faith cannot be imposed, but allegiance to Jesus can be invited by our words and lives. Take a look at Francis Bridger's *Children Finding Faith* (pp105,106) for more about this idea.

Putting it together

The faith journey for 11–14s may not be straightforward, but then it isn't for adults either. In this chapter, we've seen that:

- There's a relationship between the developmental search for identity and faith development, for example: the move away from parents with the need for self-discovery in relation to others in peer friendship groups.
- Questions, doubts and uncertainties need to be accepted and explored as part of 11–14s' growth towards independent faith.
- Dynamic owned faith is different to knowing *about* faith – this is a crucial time for faith to move from head to heart. This is potentially a very exciting time for them and us!
- Good relationships with other Christians, both adults and young people, are key in helping them to learn and own faith for themselves.
- Older and peer Christians modelling faith in their lives and words are powerful tools in bringing this age group to their own faith commitment.
- Nurture of faith in early childhood is important for commitment in adolescence.
- Many Christians see nurture and conversion as a unified process.
- It's important to be alert to how God is at work in the lives of individual 11–14s, and be ready with the appropriate encouragement or challenge.
- The faith development of 11–14s must be supported by their faith communities. This is a huge challenge for the church.
- Belonging can lead to believing.

At a critical time and opportunity for their faith growth, 11–14s' human development makes them ready to discover their own independent relationship with Jesus and make a commitment to him.

A theme throughout this chapter has been about the importance of believing community for this age group's spiritual development. But there's a problem facing Christians today: for many 11 to 14-year-olds brought up in Christian families, 'church' has dropped off the menu. Church is not a place where they feel welcome. So, what kind of 'expressions' of church are needed to help 11–14s feel part of the Christian 'story'? More about this later.

First, how can we help this age group learn faith? The next chapter looks at some approaches.

How much is your thinking in the areas discussed in this chapter informed by God's words? Here are some starting points for getting a biblical viewpoint:

A time for growth: 1 Samuel 2,3 – Samuel hears God and responds.

Doubts and questions: Luke 24:13–35 – the Emmaus journey.

Nurture or conversion?:

The Gospels – the account of the disciples' faith growth;

Acts 9:1–18 – Saul's conversion on the Damascus road.

The role of believing community: check out the stories of David (1 Samuel 16,17), Esther and Josiah (2 Chronicles 34,35) for whom the support of their believing community was significant both for their sense of identity and for the ways in which they served God.

References for Chapter Four

1   John Head, *Working with Adolescents*, p85
2   Richard Middleton and Brian Walsh, *Truth is Stranger than it Used to Be*, p183
3   John Hull, 'Spiritual Development: Interpretations and Applications', p171
4   John Hull, ibid
5   John H Westerhoff III, *Will our Children have Faith?*, pp87-100
6   Francis Bridger, *Children Finding Faith*, p105
7   Francis Bridger, ibid, p139
8   Francis Bridger, ibid, p174

… and further reading

Jeff Astley (ed), *How faith grows*

Paul Fenton, *Someone to Lean On*

Ken Edgecombe, *Will they or won't they?*

Chapter Link

For more on growing church with 11–14s see Chapter Nine.

Chapter Five – Helping 11–14s Learn

The world changes at a rapid pace. Most young people have regular access to technology and resources that adults living today only dreamt of when they were teenagers. Whether it be through interactive TV, the Internet, sophisticated computer games or video phones, the world of young people is different to the one in which most of us grew up!

This changing environment is centred on the world of communication. We are bombarded with thousands of images and sounds every day and the brain is able to process and adapt to all these different signals and absorb them. Over time, this has led to a change in the way that we acquire and assimilate information and it is important for us to be aware of that if we are going to communicate effectively with 11–14s who are a product of their time. For example, the traditional model of a 'teacher' or 'expert' passing on their knowledge is no longer the normal means of communication. Instead learning is interactive, involves dialogue and discussion, theorising and testing out theories.

Changes in learning

This changing world has significant impacts on how we choose to communicate. Young people can read but often choose not to. The sound-bite is our dominant form and adverts are often the most creative pieces of media – grabbing people's attention to drive home a message. This has implications for the methods we choose in designing learning experiences.

1 Use all the senses – I was involved in leading a holiday where the teaching room was next door to the kitchen. Often as I recall those events I also remember the smell of freshly baked bread. Strong memories are not only associated with words we hear but the way the room looks, the smell, the ambient temperature and other sensory factors. These are all influential in affecting how and what we learn. We must pay attention to all of the senses.
2 Engage in discussion – young people at this age are beginning to want to be involved in the decisions that affect them. It's not enough to hand down our wisdom; they want to be involved in discussing and shaping the direction of the activity. It's important to allow space for questions and enable them to develop their own answers as part of the learning process.
3 Vary the action – watching a modern film you will see enormous variety in the way that the action is portrayed. Even a monologue offers a variety of angles and perspectives. Most of the time a particular perspective only lasts for 20–30 seconds. We need to explore stories from a range of perspectives. In particular for those in our care who have been nurtured on Bible stories, we need to help them engage with the story afresh by looking more deeply at the characters and feelings involved.

Chapter Link

For more on school, see Chapter Three.

The learning environment

The simplest way to understand what schools are like today would be to spend a day there. Seek permission beforehand and explain clearly that you are doing this so that you can learn. For a teacher's perspective you could spend half a day in a classroom with a teacher as they teach a whole range of classes. Or you could spend some time with a class – going with them for a day to see what it is like for a young person. Notice:

- What different learning approaches are employed?
- How much time is spent listening, watching, writing and talking? Does this vary according to subject?
- How much initiative is expected from the young people and how much do they take?
- How do the young people cope with the variety of activity?
- How is discipline enforced?
- What do the young people do between lessons?
- How do the young people treat each other both in and out of the classroom?

Remember that you are a guest and so behave courteously at all times and show respect for all the rules and regulations. If you are unable to visit a school, glean some information about what young people think of school by using a simple questionnaire. Adapt this sample for your own use:

1 What is your favourite subject and why?
2 What is your least favourite subject and why?
3 What has been the best lesson you have attended in the last month and what did you enjoy about it?
4 Who are the best teachers and why?
5 What do you do at break and lunchtime?
6 How much homework do you get and when do you complete it?

All of these methods are part of the normal way that young people engage in learning – both formally and informally. One of the key differences between what is on offer by the media and what we can offer is in the area of participation. TV offers vicarious participation, but the opportunity to engage with people and relate to them face-to-face is a vital part of the learning process. We will return to the role of adults in this process later but at this stage it is important to note the vital importance of good role models and the place of relationships between young people and those who lead them.

The communication process

The most common communication media that young people encounter are TV, film, video computer games and, increasingly, the Internet. The dramatic changes in technology have had a massive influence on the effectiveness of traditional forms of communication. Didactic learning – speaking and listening for a period of time for longer than 10 minutes – is rare in the world of 11–14s. Just think about the way special effects are used in *Lord of the Rings* to create a completely different world, or the way in which even simple TV programmes develop a sophisticated framework in which to operate.

The impact of these changes has been that young people are not used to sitting and listening for a sustained period of time. Technology has meant that their 'communication diet' trains them to concentrate in different ways.

So what are the key characteristics of this technological communication?[1]

1 Multi-sensory – watching TV of course involves only two senses, hearing and seeing. However the whole design of programmes has been developed to engage those watching with the characters and storylines emotionally. The most watched programmes are the soap operas and discussion about what is happening to these characters occupies much conversation time at schools across the country every day. *EastEnders* even advertised itself at one point with the words 'Everyone is talking about it'. As a consequence many programmes have included elements of soap opera into their planning. For example, although each episode of *Casualty* may have its own story there is a bigger story that runs throughout the series and between series. The growth of 'Reality TV' relies heavily on this identification by inviting audiences to participate by voting for who to keep or who to lose – allowing viewers to participate in shaping the programme itself.
2 Multi-camera – watch any piece of media and you see the effects of technology vividly. In any given 2–3 minute clip, there are a number of camera angles employed – the close-up, the long shot, the shot from the left or the right, the wide angle. Even when a character is giving a longer speech the camera changes angle on a regular basis to keep our attention. This constantly changing landscape enables us to engage with the same character for a longer period of time because our view or 'perspective' is changing regularly.

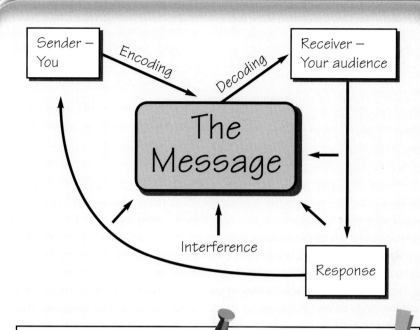

The diagram above offers a simple model of the communication process. Take some time to think about how this applies to your work with 11–14s by thinking about the following questions.

1   **Encoding and decoding** – describe the process of explaining and understanding a message. The words you choose to use when you are explaining the message to anyone is the encoding. How the young people understand those terms is the decoding. If we want to explain theological ideas we need to use simple language to avoid misunderstanding. Try to explain the concepts below using non-theological language.

- Sin
- Judgement
- Redemption
- Salvation
- Holiness

Add to the list yourself and remember that if we encode the message in the wrong words young people won't be able to decode it and understand the message.

2   **Interference** – describes the things that hinder the message from getting through. We should aim to minimise interference. There are two main types – external and internal. Take some time to list them and then look at ways of minimising them in the learning process.

External, eg noise, comfort, warmth...

Internal, eg family circumstances, peer pressure...

3   Dialogue – the world of children's TV and the world of the chat show have much in common. We no longer expect someone to come and talk to us for a long period of time while we listen. Instead we interview them – questions followed by short answers. Questions are normal and expected and allow for clarification and probing. This diet means that there is an increasing expectation that the words that people say will be challenged, questioned and examined. The authority of words no longer comes from the person speaking but because they stand up to scrutiny.

These processes should have a significant impact on the way that we communicate:

1   Using story – soap operas use story as the key means of making the audience engage with the programme. We need to think about how we use story. Investing time in how we tell the story of God's message of salvation is key. We must not simply reduce the big picture story to a series of smaller propositions to believe. Instead we want young people to see that we are involved in God's big story and plan for the world. Spike Milligan wrote a book entitled: *Hitler – my part in his downfall*. Whilst that was rather tongue-in-cheek, we need to help those we work with to see that they are not just observers of an already written story – rather they are participants in God's story. It's as if we are taking part in a play where the ending is known but we are actors on stage seeking to live our lives in a way that is faithful to the plot. We have a fantastic hope because we know that the story ends well, but there are lots of exciting opportunities to be involved and help others to participate in the story too.

2   Engaging relationally – people identify strongly with the people on TV. Although they have little hope of meeting those people, they share their struggles and joys. We need to allow young people to engage with our lives and we need to share our own stories and struggles. Taking time to talk about how God makes an impact on our lives is essential if young people are really going to engage and learn. Communication is not a simple passing on of facts. What young people are most likely to remember about their involvement with any group is who the people were, what they were like, how they treated others.

Understanding communication

Take some time to find out what are the favourite TV programmes and music for the young people you are working with. If you can find someone with cable or satellite, ask them to video some of MTV for you to watch. Finally make sure that as part of your watching you are able to see a range of adverts.

TV programmes

You will probably have a mixture of soaps, children's TV, comedy and music. As you watch them think about the following questions.

- How quickly does the action change?
- How does the programme use interaction?
- Which characters is it easy to identify with and why?
- What themes are being explored?
- How do the characters behave towards each other?

What influence are these likely to have on the way the young people you are in contact with see the world?

Music/MTV

The choice of music will vary and you may need to take some time to examine the genre and its underlying values. Again think about some questions.

- What mood is conjured up by the music?
- What themes occur regularly?
- How do the artists dress?
- What attitudes to others are expressed?
- Are the artists mainly male, female or a mixture?

What evidence do you see in the lives of the young people you are in contact with regarding the influence of this music in the way they dress, think about the world and behave?

Chapter Link

Chapter Three also has sections on TV and Music.

3 Different perspectives – we've said that using multi-camera angles offers a range of perspectives to the viewer. We need to do that in our communication too. What about examining Bible stories from a range of perspectives, eg re-telling the story of the Passion from the perspective of different characters in the story – Peter, Judas, Pilate, Thomas. This range of perspectives is particularly important if we are to help the Bible come to life for young people who may be very familiar with its content. It is also important so that they can identify with the Bible story as the living words for today rather than a book about the past.

4 Allow questions – young people will have many questions about what they have learnt in the past. As they begin to want to make faith real for themselves then they need space for dialogue. Allow regular opportunities to question and interview the key members of your church so that they see how faith stands up to scrutiny. How we deal with this will be vital. If young people get a sense of disapproval they are likely to 'clam up' and keep their questions and doubts to themselves. Instead we need to foster a spirit of enquiry that helps them to feel accepted whatever doubts and fears they have.

Learning Styles

Significant work has been done in the area of learning styles. People learn in different ways. One way of examining this has been influential in shaping thinking about the types of learning activities that we design for young people. A simple framework suggests that there are three basic learning styles.

1 Visual Learners – this does not mean young people who only learn from watching. Instead it focuses on the fact that people make sense of things by visualising them. They often refer to represent things as pictures or diagrams and may well enjoy reading, as the written word is perceived visually. Instead of lots of facts, they will be interested in concepts and big ideas. This is often reflected in the language they use too – phrases such as 'I see what you mean', 'I get the picture' or 'It's clear now'.

2 Auditory Learners – these young people enjoy language and the spoken word. They like the way that words interact and enjoy wordplay and metaphor. They enjoy constructing language to describe things – exploring the feelings portrayed by language and describing the dialogue that takes place in a story. They are gripped by good narrative and enjoy stories and storytelling. Often these people enjoy the interplay between characters in a story and are good at mimicking the accents or nuances in the speech of others.

Brain-based learning and multiple intelligences

There has been significant research done in this area. Research the Internet to discover more about this area by typing 'brain-based learning' or 'multiple intelligences' into a search engine. Listed below are some websites you might find particularly helpful.

Brain-based learning

- Funderstanding – a company of consultants targeting the youth market. There is an excellent section on theories of learning.

http://www.funderstanding.com/engaging_kids.cfm

- The Learning Forum – a number of excellent links to good summaries of current thinking. Schools Centred Initial Teacher Training for Suffolk and Norfolk.

http://www.suffolkandnorfolkscitt.co.uk/Student%20support/Learning%20Forum.htm

http://www.suffolkandnorfolkscitt.co.uk/Student%20support/Brain%20Based%20Learning%20Theories.htm

Learning styles

- Support 4 learning has a whole series of links regarding learning styles
  http://www.support4learning.org.uk/education/lstyles.htm
- A useful chart with questions to think about your own style
  http://www.chaminade.org/inspire/learnstl.htm
- There is an online questionnaire for discovering your learning style
  http://www.bbc.co.uk/keyskills/extra_m1_p01.shtml
- The University of the First Age has some examples of actual approaches and you can try out an online questionnaire
  http://atschool.eduweb.co.uk/ufa10/ufa.htm

3   Kinaesthetic Learners – these young people are hands-on people. They love to do things rather than talk about them. Whether it is in constructing things, playing a game, taking part in drama or making a collage – it is in the act of 'doing' that learning occurs. They will often feel that sitting still is a poor way to learn and love to experiment – devise theories and test them out.

It is most likely that all of us learn best by a combination of all three styles but have a preference for one style. In any group of young people you will have all three styles represented and this needs to be reflected in the way we plan and organise our activities.

The Bible is our source book which, although it is a written text, employs many of those approaches within its pages. Just looking at the prophets demonstrates that to us clearly.

Visual – the imagery employed in Ezekiel or Daniel is both complex and awe-inspiring.

Auditory – the language is rich in metaphor. We are familiar with the pictures from Isaiah of the branch of Israel, the Lamb of God.

Kinaesthetic – Hosea lives out his message by marrying his unfaithful wife. Ezekiel demonstrates his message by constructing models and living out the story.

Of course, Jesus himself employs techniques like this:

Parables – vivid stories from everyday life, which people could relate to.

Teaching – the Sermon on the Mount is an example and clearly there are occasions when people sat and listened for an extended period of time.

Practical demonstrations – the miracles of Jesus brought both relief of suffering and were used as teaching aids, eg the man through the roof, the large catch of fish. They also pointed to his deity.

Asking questions – Jesus often asked questions as part of his reply, eg whose head is on the coin?

Illustrations – when the disciples were arguing about who was the greatest he placed a child in front of them.

Dealing with questions – Jesus took time to listen to the questions that others had, never treating them as unimportant but using them as stimulus to further discussion, eg the woman at the well is a good example of Jesus dealing with the questions of others.

We need to learn to employ these techniques effectively in our own teaching programmes so that all those learning are able to engage in ways that help them to learn effectively.

The Bible and learning approaches

Think about how you would re-tell some of the incidents from the life of Jesus, making sure that you employed a range of learning approaches to reflect the three different learning styles in your group.

- Telling the parable of the good Samaritan – Luke 10:25–37
- The calling of the disciples – Luke 5:1–11
- The calming of the storm – Luke 8:22–25
- The turning over of the tables – Luke 19:45–48
- Jesus' teaching about the law – Matthew 6:17–20

In each case check back to see that you have allowed for the auditory, visual and kinaesthetic learners. Think about the questions below as a guide.

- What will we do and they watch?
- What will we prepare in advance and they do?
- What will we say and they listen to?
- What will we ask and they seek to answer?
- What will they ask and how will we answer?

Now try using the same technique for a range of familiar Old Testament stories.

- The choosing of David – 1 Samuel 16:6–13
- Joseph in prison – Genesis 39:19 – 40:23
- Joshua and the battle of Jericho – Joshua 6
- Elijah and the prophets of Baal – 1 Kings 18:20–40

Adults and faith development

As 11–14s make the transition to early adolescence, the role of adults has a significant impact on the faith development of young people. As they seek for identity and independence, they will look to adults in a different way and for different responses.

Stephen Jones, in his book *Faith Shaping*[2], suggests that adults play two significant roles – they either act as faith advocates or faith clarifiers.

Faith advocates act in ways that bring young people into contact with activities, traditions and challenges that will enable their faith to grow. These often take place as part of the faith community. This involves living lives of faith in natural ways that allow young people to both observe and participate in activities. Often Christian parents are the strongest faith advocates for their children. Paul writes of Timothy:

> I … remember the genuine faith of your mother Eunice. Your grandmother Lois had the same sort of faith, and I am sure that you have it as well. (2 Timothy 1:5)

Much of the work that takes place in Sunday school operates on a faith advocacy model. However Jones suggests that in adolescence, a second role is required.

Faith clarifiers fulfil a different role. They attempt to help young people clarify their own faith questions and give them the tools to think through the issues for themselves. They may do this using a moral dilemma, a provocative idea or look at a theological issue. The young people are then allowed to come to their own conclusions and that conclusion is respected.

Young people need both faith advocates and faith clarifiers if their faith is to grow to maturity. However at the 11–14 age range, as they begin to think conceptually, it may be that finding adults who will act as faith clarifiers is a key task for the group. Young people may feel that because their parents are strong faith advocates they do not qualify as faith clarifiers. For my own children I have greatly valued those adults who have been willing to act in that role as they look to deepen their own faith.

For myself, I've come to recognise that I prefer to work in a way that reflects faith clarification; asking open-ended questions, playing 'devil's advocate', refusing to give my own opinion but asking for theirs, making young people think through the impact of their own ideas on others. I need others who will work with me as strong faith advocates. It may be that some adults will embody both roles for young people but recognising our own strengths will help us be more effective in making sure that those we work with grow to maturity in their faith.

Adult roles in faith development

Draw a picture of a road to think about your own faith journey. What were the significant events and people who helped you as your faith developed? Mark them on the road. Choose three events and three people and think about their significance to you.

Stephen Jones suggests that there are a number of stages young people go through in adolescence as part of developing faith.

1   Experiencing – encountering spiritual feelings
2   Categorising – sorting out feelings, experiences and memories
3   Choosing – deciding what is true
4   Claiming – deciding to what I will be true
5   Deepening – maturing in the faith
6   Separating – setting aside faith for a time
7   Responding – commitment to a life calling

Can you identify these in your own faith development?

Think about your programme. How does it allow for young people to move through these stages?

Try to identify the way in which the activities you run help young people to develop in faith. Be clear about what you are trying to achieve.

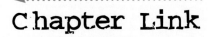

Chapter Link

Look back to Chapter Four for more on faith development in 11–14s.

Role of adults in learning

The model of working with children in church is often borrowed from our memory of school: the teacher is the expert; the learner is the empty vessel. Even if that were true (some research suggests it is a poor model) as 11–14s grow and become aware of their own faculties and ideas developing, the role of the group leader begins to change.

Young people want to have a relationship with their leaders. They do not want you to be their best friend or even an authority figure. Instead you become an adult to whom they can relate – someone outside of their family who will treat them as individuals and will value their opinions. They are interested in you as a person – your hobbies, friendships, thoughts and feelings – and they want to know that you are interested in their lives.

Rather than simply conveying information because you are the expert, your role is to design learning experiences. As this age range has increased abilities and high energy, they will need to have opportunities for those abilities to be used, that energy channelled and their opinions valued. Don't be afraid of open-ended activities that allow for a range of opinions – exploring these differing perspectives is all part of that wider learning process.

Questions are a significant learning tool for this age. Asking them to grapple with questions and knowing how to handle their questions is really important. Avoid offering simple answers to complex issues. These questions are all part of making faith personal to them. If they get the feeling that what you want is the 'right answer' then they will cease to explore but will instead look for the answer that they think you want to hear.

The Bible is our sourcebook for learning. For some of the young people in our groups it contains familiar stories they know well. What they struggle with is how these stories relate to their lives today. It is easy for us to re-tell the stories and fail to look at the issues raised by them. For example, dealing with God as a Father will not be easy if Dad is absent or abusive. In order to help young people we need to be willing to engage with their questions and allow the Bible to speak. Don't be frightened of these questions – they are a vital part of seeking to develop an integrated faith. The people in the Bible are like us – let's highlight their humanity, their failure but let's also highlight the God in whom they trusted.

Young people are looking for purpose and meaning and the overriding message of the Bible is that we can find that when we relate to the God who created us. Showing that we are part of God's plan – that as we live day by day we participate in God's story – is an essential part of helping young people to understand their value and significance.

Questions, questions

Asking the right kind of questions is key to making sure that our group engage with the issues. Take the story in Mark 10 as an example:

Closed – Avoid overuse of closed questions or our sessions revert to simply being a 'hunt' for the correct answer. Example: Did Jesus heal the blind man?

Information – Avoid Bible study simply becoming a series of comprehension questions although information questions can help young people to understand how to get information from the Bible passage. Example: What did Jesus say to Blind Bartimaeus?

Opinions – Asking questions that allow people to express their opinions will help create an environment where questioning is allowed. Although you may disagree with their opinions, expressing them is often part of thinking through and formulating ideas. Don't be shocked and, if need be, correct with gentleness. Example: What do you think it felt like to be blind since birth?

Rhetorical – Questions to which we do not expect an answer. They offer a chance to explore and present a challenge to think about an issue further. Example: Are there ways in which we are blind like the blind man?

Open-ended – Allow for a range of answers and unlock open-ended discussion. Example: How do you think people in the crowd would have responded to the blind beggar crying out?

Feelings – The Bible creates a response: we need to allow those feelings to be expressed. Asking questions that encourage this interaction will help us to discover the relevance of the Bible to our lives. Example: Are there times that we have felt as if we have been healed like the blind beggar?

References for Chapter Five

1   Jolyon P Mitchell, *Visually Speaking*

2   Stephen D Jones, *Faith Shaping*

PART TWO: NUTS AND BOLTS

Chapter Six – Approaches to Working with 11–14s

Just as there is no such thing as a typical 11 to 14-year-old, there is no such thing as a typical 11–14s group. However if we look at a group, we can pick out some common characteristics of 11–14s and so looking at a range of groups enables us to identify some helpful common characteristics of work with this age range.

On the following pages are four case studies. Although fictitious they are all based on real groups and real situations. They offer a number of ways of working and are designed to stimulate thinking about your own practices and involvement.

On the right hand pages are activities to help you think through the issues and apply them to your particular situation.

Case Study 1

Jenny is a leader in the 11–14s group at a large city centre church. The church congregation is around four hundred on a Sunday morning. The church has an evening service, which Jenny attends as well. On Sunday morning the young people come into church for the first 10–15 minutes before leaving to attend an age-specific group. Once a month the church has a family service, which the group attends, participating once a year in a family service through a piece of drama, a musical item, the readings and prayers.

A typical Sunday meeting comprises notices, a quiz or game, some up-front teaching and some time in groups where the young people are divided according to age range and gender. There is rarely any singing, as the young people don't seem to want to participate.

Jenny's main responsibilities are in leading the group of Year 8 girls when they split into small groups. She enjoys seeing the same group on a regular basis and getting to know the girls. Most weeks they look at a Bible passage together and answer questions based on the passage. She sees this as the key part of the role of the leader and looks forward to this teaching session.

Alongside the Sunday meetings, the group has a regular Saturday night social at the church hall. There are games of football, netball or hockey in the hall, table tennis and pool. There is a room just for relaxing, listening to music and chatting. There are regular special events such as bowling and ice-skating as part of this programme. Jenny attends Saturday nights whenever she can but finds that she can only manage about once every three weeks because of visiting friends or family.

Using the case studies

Strengths and weaknesses

Using a simple table (as below) take each case study in turn and identify the strengths of each youth group referred to in the case studies.

Case Study 1	Case Study 2	Case Study 3	Case Study 4

Repeat the exercise for the weaknesses.

- Think about your own experience of youth group (if you had any).
- Which of these groups was your group most like?
- What did you appreciate about it?
- What did you find difficult?
- If you are currently involved in a group then repeat the exercise thinking about that group.

Expectations

All youth groups are seeking to meet a range of expectations and whether you are a volunteer youth worker or employed, one of the challenges will be juggling those expectations.

Taking each case study in turn try to suggest what sort of expectations there might be from the following groups of people about the group.

- Parents
- Young people who attend the group
- Church leadership
- Youth leaders
- You

In each case the group seeks to juggle these expectations in the way that it organises the programme. Which expectations seem to be most important in each of the case studies?

Case Study 2

James is a member of the leadership team for an 11–16s group in a church that meets on Sunday mornings with an attendance of around two hundred and fifty. The group that he's involved in simply attend Sunday morning as part of the normal Sunday worship. No particular provision is made for the age range.

James' group meets every Friday night and has adopted a cell model for its meetings. James co-leads the cell group with a female leader, Sharon. They meet in a home for a mixture of Bible study and social time lasting around two hours. There are three groups like this and once a month they meet up for a special event at the church that includes teaching and worship. Around forty to fifty attend the monthly event and each group has around ten members. Average attendance at these groups is seven to nine. James plays guitar in the worship band that plays for the regular monthly meetings and so has regular rehearsals for that every Tuesday.

The church leadership sees this cell model as a key part of church life and James and Sharon are therefore seen to be in key leadership roles. They are very committed to seeing their group grow. They have recently looked at the idea of peer-led cells and are just beginning to implement that by identifying a leader and co-leader for the group from the 15 and 16-year-olds who attend. This will mean regular contact with these two people as they take on this role but both James and Sharon feel it is important to invest in this mentoring role.

Case Study 3

Sue belongs to a church with an average Sunday attendance around eighty to a hundred. The church has a number of families in it who attend and bring their children along. In the 11–14 age range there are eight to ten who attend. The church encourages this age range to play a full part in the life of church and so some members play in the music group; others help with Sunday school and crèche on a rota basis.

Every two weeks on a Friday night the church facilities are used to have a youth club for the over-11s and most of those who attend church with their families come along. Sue is involved with two others in helping to run this. The evening consists of a mixture of games, relaxation, food and normally ends with a short epilogue given by one of the team. The hope has been that those who attend regularly will begin to invite their friends. This has begun to happen so there is a regular group of around fifteen on any given Friday.

Activities

Below is a list of activities illustrated by the different case studies. Rank them in order according to their importance (most important 1, least important 12).

- Participation in church services
- Teaching
- Socialising and games
- Outreach to the friends of group members
- Small group interaction
- Lively worship
- Links with families
- Links with local schools
- Group members participating in church life
- Outreach to those with no church contact
- Getting young people on to church premises
- Meeting with young people from other churches

If you were to plan a programme to deliver on the most important five what would it include? How does that compare with the content and emphases of your current programme?

Formulating a strategy

Imagine that each of the leaders mentioned in the case study has written to you. They have described their group and asked if you could offer some advice to help the group grow. Write a reply to them stating what you think they should do to improve.

In the area there are a number of larger inter-church Christian events happening which are targeted at the 13+ age range. Sue is keen to encourage the older members to attend. She has taken a carload of young people to a monthly youth event attended by two hundred young people with an extended time of worship and a speaker. Although very different to what happens on a Sunday, she feels that there is great value in helping these young people see that there are other young people of their age who are also keen to learn about God and faith.

Case Study 4

Simon is employed as a youth worker for a group of five local churches and has been in the post for six months. His role is to work with the 11+ age range and help the individual churches' work to grow. He is also being encouraged to work with the local schools in making contact with young people who do not presently attend church.

On his arrival he conducted an audit of the current work and discovered that only two of the five churches had a group for anyone aged 11+. The other three churches have no one over the age of 15 attending and two or three 11–14s attending main church services. The groups that do meet are around five to eight in size and are run at the same time as the church service by a group of volunteers on a rota basis – once every three weeks.

He has made contact with the local comprehensive school and has been invited in to take school assemblies for Years 7 and 8. He has also met Christian teachers in the school and has taught two RE lessons – one on 'What Christians believe about the Bible', and one on 'Science and Religion'.

Simon would really like to develop some new work, which would be accessible for those he meets in school who have no contact with church. This would probably be a midweek drop-in youth club. He would then want to build on that with a new inter-church 11–14s group that meets on a Sunday evening for teaching. He's also keen to start some groups in the school both as an opportunity for outreach and to help support those who do attend as they seek to live out their faith in school.

Dream big dreams

Imagine your group in five years' time. What would you like it to be like? It may be that the key word is survival; it may be growth. Write a paragraph describing what you would like the group to look like. Think about the following issues.

- Constituency – mainly church background or mainly non-church background.
- Programme of activities – frequency, emphasis.
- Relationship to church.
- Leadership – how many, what skills.
- Resources – both physical and teaching material.

If you are going to realise the dream you need to plan for it so think about the following questions.

- What things do you need to do now to bring about this dream?
- What things will you need to do in a year's time?
- What things will only happen in the long-term future?
- Who do you need to talk to about this vision if it is to begin to happen?

No 'one-size-fits-all' solution

As you can see from the previous four case studies – there is no one solution for every situation. Even when people are running 'successful' groups there may be more than one approach to how church relates to this age range.

The evidence from statistical work is that the age range 11–14 is the one where young people decide to stop attending church. There is unlikely to be any one factor in that. It is no longer acceptable to see this age range as simply older Sunday school. We need to see this work as 'youthwork' and therefore plan provision accordingly. However, different solutions have been tried and proposed to prevent this leaving process. We suggest that there are four strands or emphases, which make an impact on how this youthwork develops.

1   *Involvement* – 'young people are the church of today'. They should play a full part in the life of the congregation. In this setting they will be cared for and nurtured by a range of old and young. We are all on a journey of faith together learning from each other and young people have things to give as well as receive.

2   *Outreach* – 'young people are not Christians and they need to have a real faith'. This is the time when they need to put into practice all that they have been taught as children. Much of what has gone before has been a preparation for young people to personalise their faith in early adolescence.

3   *Training* – 'young people are disciples in training'. They are our future leaders, and as such we need to develop programmes that help them to prepare for future church life in roles of leadership and participation. Opportunities for service in the present are all part of that growth and youth leaders act as coaches for this development.

4   *Youth Church* – 'young people need culturally relevant expressions of church that help them to grow'. So young people need to have an approach that reflects all that church is within their own group. Youth leaders nurture those in their care so that they take on responsibility for evangelism and nurture themselves.

Each of these emphases leads to different approaches to youth work and in particular to work with 11–14s. You will see these reflected in the case studies. It is worth taking the time to think about what the positive and negative consequences of each of these models will be on the young people you work with. It may be that in reality you pick different elements from each area and develop a pattern of working that fits your situation.

How do we show them they belong?

Stephen Croft in his book *Transforming Communities*[1] suggests that the basic building block of the local church should be a community.

'The purpose of the community when it meets is to worship God, to build relationships with one another as the Body of Christ, to learn together and to support the ministry of each member of the community in the whole of their lives.' (p71)

Think/talk about...

- What part do young people play in this community?
- How are we including them in the life of this community?
- How are we building up relationships with them?
- How do we show them they belong?

Chapter Link

See Chapter Nine for more on the question: What is church?

The picture of the early church is one that offers a vision of what church could or should be.

They devoted themselves to the apostles' teaching and fellowship, to the breaking of bread and to prayer … All the believers were together and had everything in common. Selling their possessions and goods, they gave to anyone as he had need. Every day they continued to meet together in the temple courts. They broke bread in their homes and ate together with glad and sincere hearts, praising God and enjoying the favour of all the people. And the Lord added to their number daily those who were being saved. (Acts 2:42–47, NIV)

Whatever our way of working we need to return regularly to this picture and ask ourselves how we match up with this model.

References for Chapter Six

1   Steven Croft, *Transforming Communities*

Chapter Seven – Ingredients for Growing Disciples

The question of purpose has been given much thought in the church. The popularity of the 'seeker-friendly' churches in the USA, such as Saddleback and Willow Creek, have made people look more closely at this big question. In Britain the drift from the churches has resulted in a hard examination of why churches do things the way they do.

Many companies now operate with a mission statement that seeks to encapsulate what it is hoping to achieve. We need to do the same for any area of ministry in church life, including our work with 11–14s.

Throughout this book we have made an assumption that our aim is for young people to grow in faith as disciples of Jesus. Everything that we look at, whether it be their development, our programme and activities, is designed to reflect that aim.

In the next few chapters we're going to be looking at some of the practical aspects that are part of achieving that aim. In western society we are often guilty of an unhelpful dualism in our thinking. We label things as 'secular' and 'spiritual' and think we should give more attention to the spiritual. The Bible doesn't operate with that way of thinking and Jesus announced the kingdom doesn't either.

> The Spirit of the Lord is on me, because he has anointed me to preach good news to the poor. He has sent me to proclaim freedom for the prisoners and recovery of sight for the blind, to release the oppressed, to proclaim the year of the Lord's favour. (Luke 4:18–19, quoting Isaiah 61:1,2, NIV)

Jesus dealt with moral issues (the woman caught in adultery), forgiveness (the man let through the roof), prayer (Sermon on the Mount), giving (the widow's mite) and so on... without ever making the suggestion that some issues were secular and some spiritual.

We'd like to suggest that in setting out to help young people grow as disciples of Jesus, our approach should be holistic with a concern for the whole person – every part of their life matters. At this age range we have already seen the increasing influence of peers and the role that peer pressure plays. So any programme will need to look at what is happening in the lives of young people so that we can help them to see that the good news of the gospel connects with every area of their lives.

In order to achieve this we need to see all the activities as part of a coherent programme that is holistic in its approach – not falling into the sacred/secular divide; providing a good safe social place, an opportunity for teaching and learning and a constant emphasis on the time and space needed for relationships to blossom.

The question of purpose

Knowing what your purpose is will help to make sure that you have a reason for all that you do.

Check out the vision of your church and see what are the central values and ethos. Develop a vision statement for your group by talking together with other leaders and consulting with the young people. Try to make it encompass the values and ethos of the wider church.

Saddleback Church has developed a model called 'purpose driven youth work'. Although it's only one way of looking at your work, it might provide some useful principles to follow.

'Our youth ministry exists to REACH non-believing students, to CONNECT them with other Christians, to help them GROW in their faith, and to challenge the growing to DISCOVER their ministry and HONOUR God with their life.'

(Doug Fields, *Purpose Driven Youth Ministry*, Zondervan)

Examining the five purposes of Saddleback Church and applying them in the youth work situation helps in formulating a mission statement for your own youth work. The five purposes are:

1 Worship
2 Ministry
3 Evangelism
4 Fellowship
5 Discipleship

Look at these purposes and your own youth work:

- Could you categorise your own activities according to these five purposes?
- Which of these purposes do you do well?
- Which of these do you do badly or not at all?
- What could you do to fill the gaps?
- What resources do you need to achieve this?

Developing a strategy

One useful framework to use in this task is below[1].

- Needs
- Aims
- Objectives
- Methods
- Implementation
- Evaluation

Needs: What needs do young people in this age range have? What needs do the particular young people we are working with have?

Aims: What are we aiming to achieve with this group? What is our overall purpose in running these activities?

Objectives: What specific things do you want to achieve by running your group? Look at the needs of young people you originally thought about – which of these needs are you seeking to meet?

Methods: What methods are available to us or will we organise? A Sunday meeting, midweek, youth club mainly with social time, a teaching evening, small groups, large events. We need to be clear how these different methods will help us to achieve our aims and objectives, not simply run a programme to keep the young people busy.

Implementation: What resources will we need to implement our plan? People, money, equipment, rooms etc. Thinking through all these things in advance will help what you plan to be successful.

Evaluation: How are we doing? Are we fulfilling our aims? Have our objectives been met? What has been good? What needs to change? What needs to stop?

Using this framework can be a useful way of making sure that you are adequately doing what you set out to do. It helps leaders have a sense of achievement but also places value on all the things that you do. It is important to get this right – youth work is not about numbers. It is very easy for us to place value on the things that we can easily measure, like numbers attending, even when we accept that what we are really concerned about is growth in faith.

God's strategy, your strategy

God is already at work by his Spirit calling people back to himself. So in working with young people we're seeking to work with God in this task. As we look at the Bible we see evidence of God's strategy.

Read Exodus 19,20

The order of events is significant here. God rescues his people from slavery in Egypt, leads them through the desert to Mount Sinai, then reaffirms his covenant: they will be his people, he will be their God (19:6). He takes the initiative in the relationship and our response is to be obedient (19:3). It's only then that he gives them the Ten Commandments (Exodus 20). Now you are my people, live in a way that demonstrates that. God's strategy is to take the initiative in calling people to himself.

Read John 1:10–14

When God wanted to act to rescue the world he didn't send a message or a messenger. He came as a baby – 'became flesh and lived for a while among us'. God's strategy was the incarnation. That model must influence significantly how we communicate the good news too.

Read Luke 5:1–11; 6:13; 10:1–16

Jesus didn't only go around giving the people a message, although he clearly did do this. His strategy was to call his disciples to be with him. They lived, laughed, cried, travelled and ate together. He created learning opportunities for them, gave them responsibility, rebuked them and listened to them. Jesus' strategy was to invest in the lives of his disciples – modelling the life of faith and helping them to follow him.

As we look at God's strategies outlined above, what principles can you draw out that will help you to be effective in making sure that your strategy is to work in partnership with God?

The social dimension

The move to 'big school', in whatever form it takes, offers the chance for a much wider range of interactions than has previously been accessible. New responsibilities and new opportunities abound. One of the issues that is central to this is the development of friendships. Perhaps one of the biggest factors in deciding about participation now becomes 'What are my friends going to do?' Texting or ringing them on the day of an event can significantly influence who attends.

We have already talked about the influence of peer pressure on decision-making, but one of the functions of a group for 11–14s is to counter this pressure with a counter-cultural peer group. This means that what we need to be able to offer is a programme which this age range would feel comfortable inviting their friends to.

Anyone visiting a group or coming for the first time may well be attracted by the activities on offer but is more likely to continue to come if they arrive and are able to feel part of the group. Although they might never be spoken, some of the questions that they will think about are:

- Who do I get on with here?
- Who do I like?
- Do I have friends here?
- Do these people like the same things as me?
- Can I be myself?
- Will people laugh at my mistakes?

... and a whole lot more.

We cannot explicitly answer those questions and yet the way that we organise and run all that we do has a significant impact on whether young people stay with us.

Welcome

Is the atmosphere one where people feel welcome? How does the room that we meet in look? Is it comfortable, warm, bright? Does it have items on the wall that help those attending to feel it is their room? Making sure that new people are noticed and welcomed individually can go a long way to allay fears. It can be a big thing to come to a group for the first time. Have a procedure in place to welcome new members and be in touch with them in the week prior to that visit, making sure they know details of all the events in your programme.

Transition

The time of moving to a new group is the time when young people often struggle to fit in. An informal gathering with food can offer the chance to get to know others. Encouraging regular members to welcome newcomers will help them have a role and break down the barriers. Make sure that in the early weeks of transition you take particular care not to place young people in embarrassing or awkward situations. Allow them to choose groups so that they can be with their friends. They need to feel that coming will be safe. There is a tremendous amount of fear and uncertainty about this transition stage and we need to work hard at allaying their fears.

Fun, fun, fun!

If you want your group to function as a group you need some 'glue' to make them stick together. The social dimension of your group is that glue. So you need to give attention to what you organise to help this social dimension to develop.

For most groups to function they need to fulfil three purposes:

1 TASK — groups need to know what task they are achieving. So whether it be a club night with games, a trip to bowling, a sports evening, a quiz night, a cookery course... remember to be clear about the task.

2 MAINTENANCE — groups need to be looked after. They need regular involvement from a consistent group of people. Making sure the room is available, transport to and from places, clearing up, making sure expectations are clear. All of these things are necessary to help the group function.

3 INDIVIDUAL — everyone needs to feel that their needs are being met, if the group is to function effectively.

This is a challenging remit. But it is important to have this in mind.

Think/talk about...

How might the following events fulfil the three purposes above? How would you need to organise them to create successful 'glue' for your group?

- A trip to the cinema
- 10-pin bowling
- Ready, Steady, Cook
- Weekend away
- A Beach BBQ
- A mini Olympics
- A Valentine's Day party
- Karaoke
- A drama workshop
- An evening of board games
- A quiz night
- A treasure hunt
- Other ....

Groups

We cannot relate to everyone at the same level and in the same way. That is why it is important for there to be small groups, which offer the potential for a greater depth of contact and understanding. Since friendships are so important, the young people will want to be with their friends. This is not school and so allowing them to be in groups which reflect natural friendship groups seems the best way to do this. We want people to feel happy and comfortable and friendships are a key part of this.

Fun

This age range are fun-loving. Make sure that our programme includes the chance to have fun together. Young people love to laugh and so all that we do should engage with them in a way that is fun. Of course we want them to think seriously about the issues they face, but a sense that the group they are part of is a fun place to be will be a really important factor in both keeping those who attend regularly and reaching new people.

Relationships

The relationships that are allowed to develop within a group of 11 to 14-year-olds are one of the keys to each individual developing a sense of belonging to the group. So we need a degree of intentionality about the way that our programme allows relationships to develop. Remember that peer relationships are just as important as the relationships the members have with the leaders.

However at this age young people develop relationships more easily by engaging in activity together rather than just being together to chat. The programme of activities needs to allow space for these relationships to develop. This age range also has a great sense of adventure and want to try out new things, but they want to do that in an environment where they feel 'safe' with those around them – not physically safe (although of course that is important too) – rather emotionally safe that whatever they do they will be accepted and included.

So think about what sort of activities will help relationships to develop.
- Team Challenges – activities that require the group to work together and draw on the skills of the group. Watch the TV to see examples of the sort of team games that you might be able to run and mimic them in your own programme, eg *Friends Like These*, the *Crystal Maze*.
- Food – preparing and eating food together is one of the most natural things to do. As well as providing essential fuel for any activities that you do, it provides a gap to stop, take a breather and chat together.
- Outdoor Activities – climbing, canoeing, raft building etc provide a great chance for a shared experience and lots of fun together as well as a sense of achievement. (Remember to use people who are registered with AALA as outdoor activity providers so that you stay within the law.)

Relationships between peers

If you're going to help young people to communicate with each other, you need to plan activities that will help them relate to each other. Offering opportunities to work together will help that to happen.

As a regular feature of the group try to do things that enable the young people to talk about themselves. Some possible activities are listed below, but you can devise your own.

1   Human Bingo – draw a 5 x 5 grid on a sheet of A4 paper. In each box write a phrase that relates to someone in the group.

    Eg someone who wears glasses, someone who has a birthday in October, someone who watches *EastEnders* etc.

    Now play bingo with prizes for the first horizontal line/vertical line/diagonal line/four corners and the middle.

2   Tangles – arrange the group in teams of eight or nine. Get them to stand in a circle with all right shoulders facing in. Now grab someone in the circle's right hand. Without letting go, grab a different person's left hand. Try to unravel without breaking the chain.

3   Human Sliding Puzzle – this is like those children's sliding puzzles often with a picture where you slide the tiles to remake the picture. Instead we are using people as sliding tiles. Mark out a 3 x 3 grid on the floor. Ask for eight volunteers and place them on the grid as below.

7	6	4
2	3	8
1	5	

Now they have to work together to unravel the puzzle so it is arranged in order.

1	2	3
4	5	6
7	8	

For more games to help group interaction try *Theme Games & Theme Games 2* (Scripture Union).

For more specific team building games try www.wilderdom.com/games/gamesspecific.html, or for some business games to adapt try www.businessballs.com

Of course you can't make young people relate to you or to each other. However we can model good relationship principles. Sadly many young people stop attending not because of the quality of our programme, but simply because they do not have people – either leaders or peers – who are interested in them or relate to them. As a consequence they feel like outsiders and eventually they drift away.

So how do we relate to individual 11 to 14-year-olds in our group?

Interests – what TV programmes and music do they watch or listen to? You don't have to become an avid watcher but watching occasionally helps you understand what influences them. Remember that you don't have to be like them, but you do have to like them and be interested in them as individuals.

Listening – everybody likes to talk about themselves so make sure that you allow them time to talk and you listen. You will gain a much greater insight from this than reading lots of magazines.

Questions – be interested in their lives and ask them questions about what they enjoy and do. Find out about life at school and what they love and hate about it. Demonstrate by the questions that you ask them that you have listened to them and you are concerned about what is going on in their lives.

Time – in a fast-moving world with people living busy lives, one of the most precious commodities you have available to young people is time. Although you could run a group like this on a rota basis, the danger is that the message young people get is that you are too busy to have time for them. Ideally they need to see the same faces on a regular basis so that they know you are concerned for them.

Keep in touch – if you run a programme with irregular events, send a card home to remind them about the event. Young people get very little personal post so it can be great to get a postcard addressed to them. Write a personal note on it so that it isn't just a circular. Arrange so that they get sent a birthday card from the leaders to show that you have remembered their special day.

Be yourself – if you want to relate to young people, it will involve giving of yourself. Talk about what is going on in your life with honesty. What do you do to relax? What are your interests and hobbies? Allowing the young people to get to know you will make it more likely that they will open up and allow you to get to know them.

Relationships can go sour too and at this age peer relationships can be transitory. At a time of uncertainty some of the wounds of bad relationships go very deep. Don't allow bad feelings to fester and demonstrate a consistency and fairness that shows you value all members of the group equally.

Relationships between young people and leaders

It is important when thinking about this area to be aware of the child protection issues that need to be considered.

However it is key to think about the importance of developing appropriate relationships with those in your group. Use the simple questionnaire below to discover some basic facts about your group members.

- Name
- Year at school
- School attended
- Favourite subject
- Least favourite subject
- What activities you enjoy in your free time
- CDs bought recently
- Favourite film
- Favourite food
- Favourite colour
- Favourite holiday destination
- Interests – tick all that are relevant: sport, music, drama, computer games, shopping, other…

Adapt according to your group.

Having found out this information, look for ways to talk about how these things are going. Don't always talk about school, but be interested in them as people. If they are taking part in something – a school play or sports event – could you go along to watch? Show an interest in their lives.

Chapter Link

See Chapter Eight for more on Child Protection issues.

Good relationships are fundamental to a successful group and programme. But it's not just the 'horizontal' dimension that's important. The next three ingredients all focus on the 'vertical': helping 11–14s grow in their relationship with God through Bible, prayer and worship.

Bible

The Bible isn't just a book. It is the 'Word of God'. Exciting and powerful it certainly is, but it can be a struggle to understand, communicate and learn from its truths with young people in our groups. The Old and New Testaments make it clear that obedience to the Bible's teaching is the foundation of our living for God (Joshua 1:6–8; Matthew 7:24–27). Helping 11–14s understand the Bible's authority and truth for today is essential if they are to be challenged and changed by its power (Hebrews 4:12,13).

In whatever ways we help 11–14s engage with the Bible, the aim is to help them grow in their relationship with God. Whilst teaching about the Bible may be part of the process, head knowledge is not the only goal. Our encouragement, modelling and teaching is about enabling young people to be independent Bible-users so that they can grow in their own transforming relationship with God.

Why is it important?

If you ask your group whether they think the Bible is important, they'll probably say 'Yes' – but most will probably then admit to not reading the Bible on their own daily… or ever. Why is the Bible important for them?

- The Bible says of itself that the Scriptures are given by God, the Holy Spirit – it's essential for helping all believers grow in their faith (2 Timothy 3:16,17).
- It's our 'faith story', providing the framework for all that Christians believe. It helps us know where we've come from and where we're going.
- It helps us know right from wrong and teaches us how God wants us to live. It gives Christians a shared sense of values and beliefs, which enable us to live together and demonstrate God's love to the world.
- It helps us to know Christ. He is at its centre, the connecting theme throughout the Scriptures. God's plan made clear in the Bible is held together in Jesus' redeeming work.
- It helps us to know God – what he's like and his love for us. Reading the Bible is not only for gaining knowledge about our Christian faith, but is about meeting with God in what we read and responding to what he says to us through his Word.

Meeting with God sounds pretty exciting, so what gets in the way and makes reading the Bible seem like a chore? Ask your group – and you'll probably get answers like these:

- It's difficult; it's long; you don't know where to start; it's not easy to understand; it contradicts itself;
- it's about different times in history when life was nothing like today; it doesn't seem relevant;
- there's not enough time.

How can we help?

Since childhood, you have known the Holy Scriptures that are able to make you wise enough to have faith in Christ Jesus and be saved. Everything in the Scriptures is God's Word. All of it is useful for teaching and helping people and for correcting them and showing them how to live. The Scriptures train God's servants to do all kinds of good deeds. (2 Timothy 3:15–17)

Take a look at some of these Bible verses and passages about the effect of God's Word:

- Nehemiah 8:1–12 – It changes people

- Matthew 7:24–27 – It gives a foundation for life

- Matthew 13:31–33 – Plant it and it will grow

- 2 Timothy 3:14–17 – It prepares for service

- Hebrews 4:12,13 – It's powerful, reveals the truth and challenges

- James 1:22–25 – It needs hearing and living out

- John 16:12–15 – The Holy Spirit will help us (and young disciples) understand

Think/talk about…

Why is it important to teach the Bible from childhood?

How might 11–14s get to hear and know the Bible?

Scripture Union's aims…

'… to encourage people of all ages to meet God daily through the Bible and prayer so that they may come to personal faith in our Lord Jesus Christ, grow in Christian maturity and become both committed church members and servants of a world in need.'

Source: Aims, Belief and Working Principles of Scripture Union

Helping 11–14s read the Bible

The Bible is a difficult book, written for adults. But by the time a young person is 10 or 11, parental support for personal Bible-reading is often withdrawn. How can we support and equip them so that they can become independent Bible readers for now and the future?

- Community practice
  Young people are hearing God's Word in all sorts of ways through other Christians, at church, at events and holidays – all of which help them know and strive to put into practice what God wants for their lives.

  Modelling – in lives and words – is a powerful way to convince 11–14s that regularly meeting with God through the Bible is important.

  Group reading and learning from the Bible is important for 11–14s, making use of their enjoyment of group activity and providing support for tackling unfamiliar words and ideas. Accountable relationships within the group provide the context for the Bible to shape values and beliefs.

  The affirming support of a believing community is very important for this age group's Bible engagement. As well as encouragement, it provides a safeguard against wildly individualistic understandings and, ideally, acts as a living interpretation of the text.

- Personal Bible-reading
  For many adult Christians the practice of daily Bible reading has slipped off the agenda. Consequently, an expectation of personal Bible-reading isn't passed on to young people whose faith they are nurturing. This situation is seriously damaging to the lives of the young people we serve and potentially weakening for the church of the future. Without knowledge of God's words in the Bible they have no sure way of knowing what he is like or how he wants them to live. Without understanding of the importance of building on the foundation of Jesus' teaching in the Bible (Matthew 7:24–27), young people cannot come to mature faith. Without passion for the Bible, 11–14s (and we) miss out on a sure way of meeting with God. Without communicating passion for the Bible we rob young people of a major means of growing into an independent faith. What will sustain them when we and/or a lively church is no longer available? How can the Holy Spirit bring God's words and ways to their minds in the future if those words have never been planted?

  A lack of emphasis on regular Bible-reading has, for many Christians, contributed to a lack of knowledge of the Bible, of God himself, and of the expectation that God speaks relevantly through his words in the Bible today. With a 'pick-and-choose' approach to Bible-reading, words are read out of context, leading to misunderstanding and unbalanced teaching about God and behaviour which pleases him. With no regular system for reading, the less-easy-to-read bits never get touched and there can be no gradual growth in understanding of how the whole Bible gives us a balanced picture of God and his plan for our lives.

11–14s and Bible engagement

- Model it. Talk about it. Live it out. Take the young person to the Bible and learn from it together. Be passionate about the Bible!

- Open the Bible in group times: in a short spot in a social evening, or a separate cell or home Bible study group for a longer time. Let the young people talk about it. Facilitate and clarify, but don't impose your opinions. Let the Bible speak. Why not try out the ideas on page 131 in Chapter Eight.

- Use the web. Online community groups, MSN and email – all provide means for Bible-based conversations and learning. Start your own, or take a look at Scripture Union's One Up website: www.scriptureunion/oneup

- Encourage individual Bible-reading. Support this in your group times by briefly introducing next week's readings or reviewing the last week's.

- Does your church have someone who orders and distributes Bible reading guides for all different age groups? Could your church subsidise Bible notes for your group?

- Encourage and facilitate other ways of reading the Bible, for example: paired reading, same-age cell group reading, school Christian group reading.

Resources:

One Up – Scripture Union's personal Bible reading guide for 11–14s. Tasters and group pack discounts available. Check out the website: www.scriptureunion.org.uk/oneup

YPs - Devotional readings for 12–16s from CWR

Discover – daily Bible readings for 10–13s from The Good Book Company

Word Up – group Bible investigations for 11–14s. Six titles available from SU

The Grid – Scripture Union's weekly, Bible-based teaching and learning programme for 11–14s

Absolutely Everything by Terry Clutterham. Six sessions for groups to help 11–14s get the big picture of the Bible. Available from Scripture Union and CPAS

txt msgs frm God: four brightly coloured booklets of Bible verses in text style, written by young people. Available from Scripture Union

- Starting-points

  An issue-based approach is often the preferred way in to the Bible for this age group. This puts the emphasis on starting with topics relevant to the age group (eg friends), then finding out what the Bible says about this. It's a good way of engaging the young people's interest, but if it is the only method, then it can limit understanding of the big picture of God and his plan for our lives.

  A holistic approach recognises the importance of helping young people to know the whole of the Bible – because you can't be shaped by its story, or understand your place in it unless you know the big picture. The more young people know the Bible, the more they will know God.

  As well as life-topic starting points, make sure you start with some Bible-led discussion too. Deliberately allow the Bible to set the agenda and ask us questions (eg 'How does my life measure up to what the Bible seems to be saying here?', 'What does God want me to understand from this?'). You could start with a Bible book series which you read together over several weeks. Major on one theme which catches the young people's interest, eg Job – focus on suffering, Psalms – focus on fears etc.

  Or, look at part of one Bible book and focus on different themes which run through it which are likely to get the group's interest as you tackle different passages, for example: in Genesis 37–50, life of Joseph: family, hard times, injustice, forgiveness, God's plan for your life.

  Whilst you may want to include both issue-led and Bible-led approaches, keep in mind that: the first may give young people the impression that the Bible is purely a functional book for Christians – helping you find answers, or a source of more take-it-or-leave-it options for living in our relativistic society. The danger with this is that the Bible isn't seen as authoritative or central to relationship with God. The Bible-led approach will on the other hand put more emphasis on knowing God, and the importance of obedient response to his authoritative Word.

- Not only reading

  This age group learn in and through relationships, and they like having fun together. Use whatever your group's into: music, drama, art, story, DVD, TV, technology, sport. Find a variety ways of communicating the Bible, and of allowing them to discover the Bible in whatever you do together.

  Finally, if your group is a million miles from opening the Bible together, or doing regular personal Bible reading, find any ways you can to put God's words into their lives. Walter Brueggemann talks about the Bible 'funding … imagination', and as a 'compost pile' full of 'generative' material[2]. So, be imaginative and create opportunities to get your group hearing God's words. Chapter Eight (page 128) has some further ideas on how to use the Bible in your sessions. The Bible has its own transforming power. Be its advocate. Plant it, let it grow.

Jesus used stories when he spoke to the people. In fact, he did not tell them anything without using stories. (Matthew 13:34)

Try these ways of helping your group into a Bible story or passage:

- Make up a card-matching game based around key words of a familiar story, each word written on a card, two copies of each. Spread out the cards, face down. In turn, group members turn over two cards, aiming to find a matching pair. When all the words have been revealed, get the group to tell the story, using the words as prompts. Then read it from the Bible.

- Give everyone in your group a copy of the session's Bible verses. Get them to translate the verses into text message style and text to one another. Let everyone share their versions. Look out for new perspectives!

- If it's a well-known Bible story, ask for two or three volunteers to 'tell the story' in their own words first, or act it out. Then read it from the Bible.

- Learn it yourself in advance, then 'tell the story' to the group with as much expression as possible and appropriate accents, without the Bible text in front of you. You could add interest by using cartoon drawings (don't worry if you can't draw — your group will enjoy pointing this out and maybe offer to try to improve on your illustrations!), or use relevant props (eg objects, hats).

- Give everyone a sheet with five frames, as if for a cartoon strip. Have everyone look up the Bible verses for your session. Ask them to draw a cartoon strip, with speech balloons, which tells the story or message of the verses.

Source: Word Up: Group Bible Resources for 11–14s, six titles available from Scripture Union

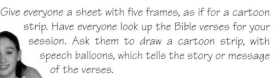

Prayer

Prayer isn't an activity in a box. It's another part of the Christian's ongoing conversation with God. It goes together with the Bible (and worship). We hear God and that prompts a response. If talking and listening to God are important for growing disciples, how do we help 11–14s pray? Some might already have a clear sense of relationship with Jesus – and have no problem in praying, on their own or out loud in your group. That's great! But lots won't find praying on their own, or especially in a group situation, easy.

Helping 11–14s pray

Remember they may find it difficult to pray in a group because:

They are not confident and don't know what to say;
They don't have a sense of personal relationship with God;
They feel they haven't got the right kind of words;
They are embarrassed (boys especially might find this difficult);
They don't feel it's relevant;
They don't know what kind of things to pray about.

Even Jesus' disciples needed to ask him to teach them to pray (Luke 11:1). So it's not surprising that 11 to 14-year-olds need some help. Every group is different, but try some of these:

- Model the value of prayer yourself in your group relationships. Refer to asking for God's help and thanking him naturally in your conversation with them. If there's a problem or need, pray with the group about it. Follow-up later with finding out how things have developed. Encourage them to pray about everyday things.
- In your group, make prayer a natural and regular part of your activities, for example: pray before going on a trip together, pray for someone who is ill, thank God for a good time together etc.
- Include times of prayer in your group sessions and be creative! Get them designing prayer sessions and activities. Depending on what the group is like, you may want to lead the group in prayer or get them praying in small groups (not twos – can be embarrassing if one person doesn't want to pray). Never insist that everyone takes part. The danger of a 'round-the-circle' approach is that people feel uncomfortable because they feel they're expected to speak when they don't want to.
- If you have a 'giggly' group – include prayer, but keep it brief.
- Include times of quiet in sessions, when you provide some ideas for prayer or some tangible things to do, hold or make as a response to God. This takes the pressure off their fear of being expected to say something aloud, takes away embarrassment, and helps those who aren't yet committed to opt out, or take some first steps in talking to God.
- Encourage people to own the group's prayer: provide a 'response' for everyone to join in with; provide a prayer for people to say together; say the 'Lord's Prayer' together.

Bible and praying

- Use/learn words from the Bible to help people pray in your group and on their own, for example: Psalms (for every feeling and need); Ephesians 1:15-18 (for other people); Matthew 6:5–14 (the 'Lord's Prayer').

- When you look at the Bible together, pray beforehand for help to hear what God is saying. Then pray about your response to what the passage teaches.

- Help the group memorise Bible verses, so that these can become a resource as a language for prayer and praise. There are some ideas for how to do this in the *Word Up* Bible resource series (Scripture Union).

- Look together at prayers and the prayer life of God's people in the Bible, for example:

  Hannah (1 Samuel 2:1–18)
  David (Psalms)
  Jeremiah (prayers throughout his book)
  Daniel (Daniel 2,6,9)
  Jonah (Jonah 2,4)
  Mary (Luke 1:46–55)
  Paul (Ephesians 1:15–23; Philippians 1:3–11; Colossians 1:3–8)

- Do your 11–14s notice anything that challenges or surprises them?

- Use a prayer from the Bible as your group's prayer – to say together or individually. Try any of the Psalms or one of Paul's from the list above.

Prayer in the Bible…

- Asking forgiveness: Psalm 51; 1 John 1:9; Matthew 6:12,14,15.

- Praying for ourselves and others: Matthew 7:7–11; Ephesians 6:18–20; 1 Timothy 2:1–3

- Giving praise and thanks: Psalm 145; 1 Thessalonians 5:16–18

For a programme outline to help your group learn more about what Jesus said about prayer, including the model prayer he taught his disciples, take a look at the series in *Word Up: How to be Happy*, Session 4, written by Terry Clutterham. *Word Up* titles are available from Scripture Union.

- Keep a group 'diary' of things prayed for and record how you see God answering.
- Encourage them to talk to God in their personal lives anytime, anywhere – it's not something that must be done quietly in a darkened room! – thank him, ask for help, ask for forgiveness.
- The 'sorry, please and thank you' model might still be a useful way of helping them know what to say to God. Youth Alpha for 11–14s (see alphacourse.org) uses the 'teaspoon' model or 'tsp': Thanks, Sorry, Please.
- Build in Bible-teaching about prayer.

Questions about prayer

Like Bible-reading, prayer for some 11–14s might seem like one more of those things that Christians are meant to do, but they are not quite sure why, or what the point is.

What do you pray for? Jesus' teaching shows that prayer is first about asking for what God wants – in his big plan, and in his plan for our lives – not necessarily what we want (Matthew 6:5–14). The 'in my name' clause in John 14:13,14 is important. It makes us ask questions like:

> 'Do I honestly think this is what Jesus wants?'
> 'Does it fit with what I know of God's will in the Bible?'

Can I talk to God about anything? Yes! Unlike parents to whom 11–14s might not always want to tell everything on their mind, God won't be shocked and won't ground you. But like a loving parent (Matthew 7:11) he does want the very best for us. So, whilst it makes sense to think about what God's take is likely to be on our prayers, we can tell him, in our own way, about whatever is on our mind (eg fears, guilt, thanks to him for good things). Take a look at Psalms.

Why doesn't God always answer my prayers? When we bring a shopping list to God it might seem that he doesn't always give us what we want. Matthew 7:7–12 makes it clear that God does answer our prayers, but in ways which are good for us and in line with his will.

Be ready to explain that, unlike God, we don't have the big picture perspective that he does. When it feels that God's not answering – David felt like this in Psalm 13 – we simply have to hang on and keep trusting our good and loving God to do the right thing for us. This is hard. Explain that it's one of the reasons why it's so important that we make sure we have support from one another – to help us keep going through the dry times.

Every group, and individual members, will vary. Be ready to help your group develop their prayer lives as they learn to listen to what God is saying to them.

Problems with prayer

What they say…

- I don't think I'll get round to this…
- I don't know what words to use.
- How do I hear God?
- Why praise God?
- My mind's all over the place!
- God isn't answering.
- Why say sorry?
- What do I do when God speaks?
- I'm struggling to keep going…
- What do I pray if someone gets really ill?

Source: *You and God: The Essential Prayer Diary* is written by Elaine Carr especially for younger teenagers. It's a great book to help them get their heads around prayer and start talking — and listening — to God.

Resources for prayer for 11–14s:
You and God: The Essential Prayer Diary, Elaine Carr, Scripture Union, 2004

Sue Wallace, *Multi-Sensory Prayer*, Scripture Union, 2000

Dave Gatward, *Connect to God*, Scripture Union, 2004

David Gatward, Kevin Mayhew, *Time Out (a collection of kickstart prayers for teenagers)*,

David Gatward, 2002 Kevin Mayhew, *It's Me Again, Lord*, 2002

One Up website Prayer Zone: A place for 11–14s to exchange prayer needs and give praise for God's answers.

Whatever happens, keep thanking God because of Jesus Christ. (1 Thessalonians 5:18)

Worship

Worship is at the heart of an individual's faith response to God – which results in praise, adoration and is demonstrated in a life given in service to God (Romans 12:1,2; Isaiah 6:1–8). It is inextricably connected with our response to God's words in the Bible, and with prayer. There's a danger that if we imply, unintentionally to young people, that it is limited to singing and music – which are often part of our worship – we limit their response to God.

Some points to think about as you build 'worship' into your programme:

- Be careful to help your group have a wide understanding of worship. Worship isn't just about the ten minutes (or longer) given to singing in your session. Worship needs to spill over into the whole of their lives.
- Different churches have very different styles and practices. People are different too (outgoing, emotional, reserved etc). Whilst you'll be directed here by the beliefs and culture of your own church, remember that individuals are different. Lack of enthusiasm about worshipping in a particular way doesn't mean that someone isn't making a response to God. Respect that.
- This age group can get very emotional. Be careful that any 'times of worship' don't wind the group up so that emotion and tiredness are speaking, not God. (Watch out for late nights!)
- Don't embarrass this age group by insisting they sing – some (especially boys) hate it. But music is very important for most teenagers. If you want to encourage them in praise – use music they enjoy listening to. This might be songs that your whole church enjoy singing together, but it might be a Christian band on CD which their age group enjoy. Encourage them to listen to CDs with lyrics that are faith-building and biblical.
- Music's a great way of remembering truths about God and for giving young people a language to praise God when they're away from Christians. Again, lyrics are a good way of communicating biblical messages.
- Be careful not to give the impression that it is only through corporate 'times of worship' that God speaks. They may not be available to sustain the young person's faith next week, or in a few years' time. Remember that God does speak through the Bible, and worship is a response to hearing its message. Choose songs and creative activities that will keep God's words in their hearts and minds.
- Relationships are important. People need to feel comfortable together to worship God.
- Worship can either be a great way of prompting growth or, if it's just compartmentalised, unrelated-to-life singing and emotion – a great turn-off.

Bible, prayer and worship are central to a believer's relationship with God. Our ongoing nurture of faith will mean creating opportunities for these, as means of helping 11–14s respond independently and personally to God. But Christian faith isn't just about the inner spiritual life; all of these three ingredients result in faith being demonstrated in witness and service.

Thanksgiving, praise and worship...

Giving thanks or gratitude is a natural human response when things are going well, although we often forget! Build on opportunities arising out of your group's everyday lives to say 'thank you' to God, for example: achievements, good times, food, one another. Be creative! Write or draw prayers, use clay or craft materials and make music. Helping them direct their thanks to God encourages their recognition of his work in their lives and dependence on him.

Praise is telling God, Jesus and the Holy Spirit the great things we know about them. Most in your group probably know quite a bit about God. Encouraging them to voice 'praise' (songs can be a good way, if speaking your own words is embarrassing) helps them understand more about God and come to know him. For some, praise will be a joyful response to the God they know, expressing how they feel about him.

Worship is bigger than praise, expressing submission to God as King of our lives. There can't be true worship without real desire to obey God and live life for him. True worship will be expressed in everyday living. Not all your young people will be ready for this. Don't ask them to say or sing 'confessional' words to God which aren't true for them. 'Non-confessional' songs on the other hand, proclaim truths about God so that all the group can join in meaningfully. However, witnessing the 'worship' of peers (as well as of the adult congregation), could be significant in helping some young people to own Christ as Lord for themselves. Don't be afraid to challenge 11–14s to think about whether they want to sing the words. It could be a tipping point for their growth into relationship with God. But don't let a 'time of worship' exclude some who feel this is not for them.

Service

We have seen already the energy and abilities that 11–14s possess. Getting involved in the life of church is one way of channelling that energy and using those abilities. The re-emphasis on 'evangelism through service' in recent years is not one that should be restricted to older teenagers. Significant learning takes place through participation rather than listening.

Think about these three areas:

1 Service in the group – rather than members of your group being consumers of a product, intentionally involve them in practical tasks that help the group run. Setting up for an event, helping set up the room/clear away, running a tuck-shop or decorating the room that you meet in. Involve them in planning an event, preparing a sketch, leading prayer, sharing their story, reading a Bible passage and so on. Participation in all these areas will help young people to feel this is their group.

2 Service in the church – it is easy for many jobs in the church to be reserved for adults. But young people have all sorts of gifts and perspectives that enhance church life. As well as involving them in traditional roles such as leading the prayers, running a youth service, reading the Bible, performing a sketch or a song, helping with crèche or younger groups, think about how they might be full participants in all roles in church. What about including young people as members of the welcome team, providing drinks after a service, members of the church council, aiding during the administration of Communion? If we see young people as integral to the church family we should seek to use and develop their gifts through our current structures.

3 Service in the wider world – as young people become aware of the wider world, they also have a strong sense of justice. Let's encourage it, not stifle it, and provide ways of acting that will mean that they feel able to make a difference to the things they see. Get involved as a group in partnering with a relief agency. Possibilities include sponsoring a child, providing practical help, sponsored events. Develop a partnership with a youth group overseas and look at ways of keeping in touch that will be of mutual benefit. But don't forget the issues closer to home. Offer practical help – perhaps helping the elderly with shopping or gardening. Events like Festival Manchester and Soul in the City demonstrate that service is a key way for young people to demonstrate their love for God and others.

There is great value in doing this together. In the past the Christian Union group that I helped to run had its own house-party centre that was available to other groups. The regular maintenance was done by groups of young people, which gave them a sense of ownership of the centre.

All these opportunities are aimed at getting young people to participate in service as an integral part of expressing their commitment to God – whole-life discipleship.

Getting your hands dirty

Some ideas to explore

1 Scripture Union International

We work in over 130 countries so why not think about making links with SU in another part of the world. For example, link your group and another group in Africa or South America. Check out the international website for more information:

www.su-international.org

2 Tear Fund

Check out ways of getting involved in making a difference to the world's poor. Check out their website:

www.tearfund.org/youth

3 World Vision

With well-established events like 24-hour famine, this organisation is worth connecting up with. For information about the famine or sponsoring a child, check out:

www.worldvision.org

Witness

If you are a regular churchgoer in today's society you are in a minority. You are different. But being different is one of the things that 11–14s don't want to be! They want to fit in, to belong. So the challenge of speaking out about their faith at school or with their friends socially is linked to the fear of non-acceptance and being different.

So how do we help young people in their witness when they worry that 'I won't know what to say', 'My friends will laugh at me', 'I'm not sure about some things myself', 'I'm not good enough'?

Some young people face ridicule, verbal abuse and even persecution because of their faith. For others these responses are more imagined than real but the fears are genuine and coping with those is an important part of this age range. It is only with a greater degree of maturity and security in their identity that they can say 'I will believe this no matter what other people think about me'.

There are at least three things that will help them to grow in confidence:

1   Deal with their questions and doubts honestly – in your sessions don't always deal with what we should believe or how we ought to live. Admit the discontinuity between what we say and what we do. Allow space for questions and do not be shocked when they admit that they have doubts and don't believe what their parents believe. Admit that there are times when you struggle, fail and don't have all the answers but help them to see that is OK. Most importantly of all don't treat their questions as trivial and unimportant but realise that these are genuine concerns.
2   Teach them practical ways of both talking about their faith and living for God – presenting the Christian life as a challenge and an adventure rather than a set of rules to follow and things to believe. They are much more likely to respond to this challenge and 'go for it' than to follow a ritual.
3   Organise well-run, welcoming and fun events that they will feel comfortable bringing their friends to. It needs to be cringe-free so be aware that a low-key event with a chance to do things together is more likely to appeal than an in-depth Bible study or an evangelistic talk with a strong appeal. These have their place, but may not be the best place to start with this group.

Of course young people are not the only people who struggle with their witness. Be honest about your own struggles and be willing to talk honestly about how you are involved in witnessing to those around you.

Remember not everyone is an evangelist – speaking clearly and boldly about what they believe. Make sure we don't impose expectations on young people that are unrealistic (and that we don't expect of adults). Emphasise that young people can be a witness simply by living their lives alongside friends and family.

Voluntary School Christian Groups

Encouraging the growth of school Christian groups is a key part of Scripture Union's ministry – there is even a section of the Scripture Union website devoted to it. Check out www.scriptureunion.org/schools for regularly updated resources including information about:

- Starting and running a school group
- Praying for schools
- Building church–school links
- Assembly ideas
- Thematic outlines for use in school groups

There are also books and a CD-ROM particularly designed to help equip those leading groups – teachers, youth leaders or student-led groups: www.scriptureunion.org/re-source

Simon Barker and Bruce Lockhart, *Running Christian Groups in Secondary Schools*, Scripture Union, 1999

Flatpack: Ready-to-go Assembly Ideas for 11–14s, Scripture Union, 2004

Listed below are descriptions of young people and their different responses to their school Christian group. Look at each in turn and discuss what you might do to encourage them to participate in their group.

- Ian's the son of your church leader. He gets a lot of teasing at school about that and chooses to avoid other Christians at school because he thinks that the teasing will get worse.
- Helen regularly goes to the group and has a great deal of Bible knowledge. As such she is always first to answer the questions and prevents others from speaking, or corrects them when they say something wrong.
- Peter says that he doesn't need to go to the Christian group because his church youth group is really good.
- Simon keeps his weekend life and his school life apart. He doesn't want anyone at school to know that he attends church and wouldn't go within a mile of the Christian group.

Taking school seriously

Many schools have school Christian groups, which meet for the express purpose of enabling Christians in school to support one another. Encourage the young people in your group to find out who the other Christians are in their school. There might be a Christian teacher who can offer support or a local youth worker who has contact with the school. Knowing that there are other Christians around can be a tremendous encouragement and enable people to tell others about their faith.

Christian groups provide interaction with a wider range of church backgrounds than young people would normally meet. This helps them understand they are part of a bigger family and the importance of the wider church. It is also a place for young people to meet older teenagers who can serve as good role models for living as a Christian at school.

It's very easy to run our programme in church-based youthwork without ever taking account of the fact that for most young people where the 'rubber hits the road' is at school. At this age young people are increasingly aware of their own failings and faults. Telling them 'Your lives might be the only Bible some people will ever read' might be true but often leads to a feeling of guilt and inadequacy rather than a greater motivation to witness. So what can you do to help them to be consistent in this area?

- Illustrate from school life – tell stories about faith at school – both successes and failures. This can be done by leaders being willing to talk about their own experiences but also by encouraging young people to be honest about how they feel about school.
- Apply the teaching in a school situation – whether you are using case studies, role play or simply talking about how to put faith into practice, use illustrations that take school seriously. What do you say in an RE lesson, to your friends, to those who are anti-Christian, in the science lesson? The group should be a chance to work these issues in a 'safe' environment.
- Pray for schools – both as part of your group but as part of the prayer life of your church, make prayer a priority. Maybe a church house group could adopt a school as their prayer focus. A regular feature praying for schools, teachers, pupils as part of a church service will make sure that school is on the agenda.
- Give time – get involved in supporting the school in practical ways. Your church building could be used as part of Religious Education for a school lesson. Get involved with the Parent Teacher Association to help fund-raise for the school. There are opportunities to be involved as a governor – an opportunity for great influence but it will involve significant time. Knowing that your church sees schools as important will help young people to see its significance.

Ministry to schools — what your church can do

Try to raise your church's awareness of schools.

Starting a prayer group:

- advertise it widely
- tell the school what you are doing
- arrange a suitable pattern of meetings
- try not to become exclusive
- pray for specific things
- keep confidences
- persevere

Praying in church:

- include schools in the intercessions
- mention news from schools in church bulletins
- pray for church members who are in schools

Churches can offer people:

- teachers, pupils, parents and others who are already involved
- support for Christian governors
- classroom assistance, eg reading
- adults to assist with trips and camps
- specific counselling and support
- people with specialist expertise for the curriculum
- practical help around the school — gardening?!

Churches can offer resources:

- use of church building
- books
- ideas and resources for RE
- help with school groups (Christian Unions)
- after school clubs (homework as well as Christian groups)

Adapted from Emlyn Williams, *The Schools Work Handbook*, Scripture Union, 1996

Check out *Generation to Generation* (Scripture Union) for more practical ways of getting involved in your local schools.

References for Chapter Seven

1 *SPECTRUM Youth Training Manual*, The National Christian Education Council, 1989, Session 5
2 Walter Brueggemann, *Texts Under Negotiation*, pp10,19,61,62

Chapter Eight – Planning the Programme

Programming – the long-term

It would be very easy to simply try to be spontaneous with our programme for a term, a half term or even a month. But if we are going to be clear about achieving our aims we need to plan ahead. Since young people go to school a programme for a term seems a logical approach. You might find that half a term (normally six to eight weeks) is all you can manage. As well as helping you to see where you are going, a plan will also help to see what resources are needed and who is taking responsibility for what each week. A blank programme is on the page opposite for you to use.

Remember that most young people do not have a filofax or use an electronic organiser. Although they are spontaneous, they belong to families who have other commitments and they participate in a whole range of other activities.

Aims

It will help if you know what the main aims are for the term. At the start of a school year or after any influx of new people, you need to take account of the needs of these newcomers, making sure that they know what is going on, explaining things clearly and being explicit about expectations. As the group becomes more established and the young people settle in to the group, you will then be in a position to judge their needs most effectively.

Teaching theme

Choose a banner title that sums up your aim and then build your teaching around that theme. Even if you choose to work your way through a book of the Bible or a series of stories, try to develop a framework that lets them hang together. Don't be afraid of raiding titles from contemporary TV, music or film to hang ideas around.

Weekly focus

Within our programme we need to be clear about what the focus of each week will be. It's easy to dot around the Bible, but probably more helpful to stick to one piece of the Bible as our main focus, drawing on other resources as needed. The other items in our programme should have a clear link to our teaching and we need to be explicit about linking all those different areas together.

Describe what you would like your group to look like in two years' time.

Below is a sample term programme for you to use and adapt for your own use (a sample weekly outline is on page 133).

OVERALL THEME: Getting to know God

Week	Day/Date	Timings	Theme	Responsible	Notes
1	Fri 11	7.00-9.00	Pizza and games night	John	Meet @ 6.45 with cars
	Sun 13	10.45-11.30	What is God like?	Sue	All to set up @ 10.15
2					
3					
4					
5					
6					
7					
8					
9					
10					
11					
12					

Meeting socially

Putting your programme together means taking account of the whole programme, so make sure that you include that in your thinking. Be aware of half-term dates, school holidays, special occasions in your own church and special events in your area. By building in those occasions and attending them together, you can help build a sense of group identity. It is important to get a balance here so that there is a mixture of events that allow the different young people to participate. Always focusing on sport or music will alienate some. You also need a mixture of active events with lots to do and opportunities to relax together. Bear in mind the developmental stages of members in the group – 11-year-old boys will want to be doing and are probably not interested much in the girls; 14-year-old girls will be more likely to want to be together and will certainly want to talk about the boys.

Don't forget that one of the best ways to find out what young people would like to do is to involve them in the planning process.

Getting a balance

Variety is a key element for a balanced programme. Using video every week can get dull. Whilst maintaining a core element to provide continuity, look to vary your methods from week to week. There is a wide range of methods you can employ, look to use them well and appropriately: quizzes, games, talks, video, drama, art, clay, writing prayers, case studies, working in groups, working alone, discussion, role play…

The list could be even longer, but the key issue is to use a range of approaches to keep your programme fresh. Remember what we said about learning styles (Chapter Five) and allow this to have an influence on your programme. Try the ideas opposite to enliven your Bible input.

Reviewing the term

If you want to make sure that you are hitting the target, then it is important to build in a review process. Asking a few simple questions on a regular basis will enable you to a) be encouraged as you review things and b) identify areas of improvement.

- What went well and was encouraging?
- What went badly and was a disaster?
- What areas were weak and could be improved?
- What areas were strong and could be built upon?
- What did the group enjoy most?
- What did the group enjoy least?
- Was there anything missing from our programme?

Don't forget that one of the best sources for evaluation is the young people themselves. It is important to include their perspectives as part of the evaluation process. Ask their opinions regularly – through questionnaires, conversations and involving them in the whole process. But remember that individuals don't have the full picture and will not always be as inclusive of the wider needs of others, so you will need to make sure a range of views are included.

Chapter Link

Look back to page 115 (Chapter Seven) for other Bible ideas.

Try these ideas for varying use of the Bible in your sessions:

Photostory: Ask the group to act out a Bible story or parable. Appoint a 'director' and 'camera person'. Using just one roll of film, photograph the story. Get the group to write captions and speech bubbles for the photos. Mount their work to show to the rest of the church.

Scribblearound: Write out your chosen passage and give each person a copy. Encourage them to write their thoughts around the passage, underlining words, circling things, putting ticks by things they agree with, question marks by things which need further explanation, comments next to words or phrases. Make a very large copy of the passage with plenty of white paper surrounding it. Get the group to transfer their individual comments on to the large one, if they want to – a chance to see the Bible as a 'community book'.

Magazine Cut-Up: In groups, create collages which bring out the theme, or most memorable part, of the passage. Make it into a game by setting time limits on choosing the pictures, assembling the collage and writing a caption.

Write a Rap: Encourage your group to rewrite psalms or parables as raps, songs, stories – anything that will evoke a response from them. Find a way of 'performing' them to a wider audience (eg church congregation).

Get to the Place: Actually go to the kind of place mentioned in the Bible verses if possible – a busy street, a tree by a stream, a river, the seaside etc. Maybe include your Bible time with your outing. 'Being there' and using the scenery and atmosphere can help put people right in the picture!

Programming – a week at a time

Having a broad plan is great, but week-by-week it is important to know who is responsible for what area of the programme. This is really important if the leaders are going to function effectively as a team. Some things that you plan will require considerable preparation and a weekly plan should help to identify those, so that everyone is aware of the time commitment involved in running a particular part of the week's event.

Some practical areas to be aware of:

Forward planning

Although some will feel comfortable just being asked to lead a group, open in prayer, give a notice or run a game of football 'on the spot', others prefer to know in advance so that they feel in control of the situation. For every activity in each week, outline what is needed and make sure that if other leaders need to do something, they know in advance. A quick phone call or email can save a lot of unease or embarrassment.

Resources

If we are going to use a variety of methods then we are going to need a variety of resources. Knowing where these resources are available will help things to run smoothly. It may be that equipment needs to be booked in advance, moved from somewhere else or brought from home. There will also be a number of items that you need on a regular basis. Keeping a stock of these items and bringing them every week will help.

Every Week	Occasional Use
• Bibles (one each) • Pens/pencils • Paper – various sizes up to A1 • Marker pens – mixture of colours • Scissors • Glue (Pritt sticks) • Chairs and tables	• Video and TV • Laptop computer • CD player • Overhead projector • Flipchart and pens • Musical instruments • Paint • Clay • Extension cables

Add to these to reflect your own situation.

Responsibilities

Make sure that your weekly schedule clearly indicates who has responsibility for what area. I often find that pairing people up helps provide both support and accountability, to make sure that tasks are completed.

Setting up and clearing away

If any event is going to run smoothly there are a number of 'behind-the-scenes' roles. These tasks are often unseen and sadly unappreciated. Noting these on your weekly programme highlights their value and importance. It also gives a message to the young people about the importance of what you do. If young people arrive at an event whether it is social or teaching, they want to feel that this is well-run and organised and so worth attending and participating in.

A sample blank timetable for each week is below. Copy to all leaders to make sure everything is planned. The first event has been completed as an example.

WEEK …

Events this week 1 *Cinema Trip*   Day/Date *Friday* Timing *Meet@6, back by 10*
Leaders available *John, Tim, Joan, Helen*   In Charge *John*

Events this week 2   Day/Date   Timing
Leaders available   In Charge

	Details	Responsible	Timing
Setting up			
Bible passage			
Activities			
Equipment			
Outline programme			
Clearing away			
Other Items to consider			

Using technology

Young people are growing up in a media-saturated world. It would be easy to fall into the trap of using modern technology just to appear trendy or be cool. However, wise use of the technology can enhance learning so we should consider how to use it effectively.

Film and TV

The Simpsons is one of the most watched television shows around the world. It has been estimated that 1 in 10 shows has a religious dimension. Many soap operas tackle issues such as marriage break-up, violence in the home, sexuality, cheating, law-breaking on a regular basis. Films offer alternative ways of viewing the world and alternative stories for making sense of the world.

There are two challenges that we face as a result of this:

1   Young people are being presented with a view of the world through television that sometime contradicts our biblical view of the world.
2   Young people's conversations and issues are shaped by what is going on in the world of celebrity.

It is important that in seeking to communicate we make connections with this world of young people. We can do this in a number of ways.

*   Using clips from TV or film to illustrate themes and ideas. A short clip as an introduction to a theme or to illustrate the point we are trying to make.
*   Highlighting the values that underlie the films and television shows they watch and helping young people to critique these.
*   Raiding the culture for ideas for activities to do with young people. There is a note of caution to sound here. Be aware of the underlying value of some of them. For example, the underlying value of many game shows is greed. However running your own versions of common shows will help to make connections with their world.

Music and fashion

As young people develop at this age, so do their musical tastes. It is likely that a whole range of musical genres will be represented in your group and this will lead to members dressing differently as a way of expressing their individuality. They may also listen to things that they think their parents (or even you) will find objectionable. This is all a normal part of seeking an identity.

Whilst you can't assume they will all like the same music, you can look for ways of using a range of musical styles to connect with their world. Look for songs with themes of searching for meaning or songs that enable you to empathise. Be willing too to help young people to critique the lyrics of the music they listen to, but be aware that for some it is the style that is important, not the content.

The type of music they listen to often influences what young people wear, but remember not to judge by outward appearance. This is all part of them trying to establish a degree of independence.

Ideas for DVD/video, television and music
If you want to use these as a regular feature in your group, check out the lists below.

Books
Doug Fields and Eddie James, *Videos that Teach 1, 2 and 3*, Zondervan, 1999, 2002, 2004

Bryan Belknapp, *Blockbuster Movie Illustrations and More Blockbuster Movie Illustrations*, Group Publishing, 2001

J John and Mark Stibbe, *The Big Picture and The Big Picture 2 – Finding the Spiritual Message in Movies*, Authentic, 2003

Steve and Ruth Adams, *Music to Move the Soul*, Authentic, 2003

Websites
There are a limited number of free video clip suggestions available.

The source for youth ministry
http://www.thesource4ym.com/videoclips/r-moviesbyjon.asp

Group Publishing's youth ministry site
http://www.youthministry.com/discussion/homevideo/index.asp

Some sites offer vast amounts of resources but require you to subscribe. Two of the best are http://www.ministryandmedia.com/ which has videos, TV, films and music ideas and http://www.movieministry.com/

Christian Video Licensing Europe
If you are going to show clips as part of your work you'll need a licence. Details and an application form at http://www.cvle.com/

Videos
There are some excellent video resources produced by One Small Barking Dog http://www.osbd.org. In particular check out 'Right Here, Right Now' and 'Walking the Dog'.

Worship ideas
There are some good links to a whole range of visual resources on the alternative worship site http://www.alternativeworship.org

Youthwork magazine has ready-to-use video, music and worship ideas in their resources section every month.

The Christ we Share produced by CMS includes a series of images of 'Christ' from around the world with ideas for how to use these in a group.

Computers and video games

Most young people have access to a wider range of computing technology than most of us dreamt of. Homework may well expect them to have a high degree of computer literacy and computers are being used on an everyday basis in the classroom.

Computers and the use of PowerPoint offer the opportunity to increase the sophistication of audio-visual presentations. Too often we use a computer simply as a technological blackboard – lots of text and nothing more. This doesn't really enhance the presentation. Look for ways of combining the visual with your text. But don't get carried away: over-use of animation can become more of a distraction.

Video gaming is often a solitary activity, but look out for games that involve interaction – 2-, 4- or even 8-player games – and maybe use these activities as part of your social programme.

Increasingly a video projector is a useful tool for groups, but it is really only necessary if you have a group larger than 20. You'll also need to have some way of connecting to a hi-fi or CD player for the audio track if you want it to be heard by all. It's possible to buy inexpensive gadgets to display the computer screen on a television, which will be adequate for a small group.

Mobile phones and the Internet

As well as access to a whole range of information, the Internet offers a way for young people to interact with each other in a way that is different to previous generations. Combine this with instant text messaging and a whole new world opens up.

The ability for young people to connect with their peers using technology is almost taken for granted. It's a private world and is a chance to participate in a virtual community. There are some significant child protection issues (see later in the chapter) to be aware of when we seek to use this technology, but it's a useful ministry tool.

Email offers a way of communicating with your group on a more regular and instant basis. MSN messenger enables online conversations to take place and young people to interact with each other even though they can't meet. Texting means that young people can keep each other up-to-date and stay in touch even when away from home.

Look for ways of using this technology – regular email updates, reminders of events, a programme of reading the same passages as a group and sharing online are just three examples. Be creative.

However there are some cautionary notes to observe:

- Young people see this kind of communication as their space and may not appreciate adults 'muscling in'.
- Remember that although you may be emailing a young person, access to home computers isn't limited to young people. Treat everything you do as public and be aware of how it could be misunderstood or misinterpreted by parents who may also read it.

Look back to Chapter Three for more information on TV and electronic media.

Practical advice on using technology

Keep it simple. The group size has a significant impact on the technology needed:

Group<10: Normal domestic televisions and a portable tape/CD player will provide a large enough picture and loud enough volume for this size of group. Using a 17-inch monitor will provide a big enough screen size for a computer if you are using pictures.

Group >10 but <20: A large (bigger than 24-inch) TV will be adequate but it is likely that the volume will distort. Look at ways of taking the output from the audio of the TV into a largeish tape/CD player, these tend to have a higher wattage than TV speakers. Think about investing in a device that allows you to display your computer on a TV.

Group >20 but <40: Use multiple TV screens or a video projector. The volume from most projectors is too low to be of any use so you will need to connect the audio signal to a large tape/CD player – 40-50 w output. For computers the data projector is the best option.

Groups >40: As well as a data/video projector you will need some form of amplification for the sound. A small portable PA system. A decent screen will be a sound investment.

Presentation issues: No matter how good your technology, bad positioning will detract from its use. Place equipment so that all can see and so that you will not be leaning across it or standing in front of it. For large events think about projecting from behind the screen or supporting the projector from the ceiling to avoid shadows being cast.

Remember technology is your slave not your master – good technology will not make up for bad preparation or organisation!

Discipline

Most young people respond well, in structured situations, to discipline. However it is at this age that young people will want to push the boundaries. They want to feel trusted although they sometimes let us and themselves down. How can we allow young people a greater degree of freedom whilst continuing to operate safely?

A discipline regime that is too strict will lead to rebellion, with young people seeking to push the boundaries and break the rules. A regime that is too relaxed will often result in chaos as young people will not know what is acceptable behaviour and so will sometimes act inappropriately and sometimes unsafely.

We are *in loco parentis* and the care of other people's children should be our primary concern. Following some simple principles will help us as we seek to operate a group.

Make the boundaries clear

There needs to be an agreed set of standards that leaders agree upon and young people are aware of. All leaders need to act consistently in applying these standards. You also need to know what action you will take if someone oversteps the mark. You will need to be seen to be fair and give clear reasons for rules.

Be in control

Good preparation is often the key to good discipline. Make preparations beforehand and arrive before the young people so you can take control from the start. Have everything planned and laid out so it is easily accessible and you are free to deal with incidents as they occur. Raising your voice often gives the impression of being out of control so speak firmly at your normal volume.

Never ignore unacceptable behaviour

Deal with some persistent trouble-makers privately in order to get to the root of the problem. If you ignore them you will simply give permission to continue to behave badly. If necessary remove trouble-makers from the group, allowing space for a cooling off period and stopping them playing to an audience of their peers. Doing this will help restore a more balanced perspective.

Treat everyone equally

Young people will be very conscious of any favouritism. Even if a young person behaves badly we should remember God values them. It might be that there is an underlying reason for the behaviour. Treating them as individuals and being concerned for their situation will help you to be consistent and fair in your discipline.

Responsibility and accountability

Appeal to young people's sense of responsibility and the need to respect one another if they want to be respected themselves. Demonstrate that you trust them. Help them to see the consequences of their actions and to act considerately towards others in the group. As part of understanding the rules, talk with them about what they mean and help them to be involved in upholding them. Get the group to agree a set of rules themselves. They are often much more likely to 'police' each other by pointing out when the rules are broken, if they have agreed them together.

No discipline seems pleasant at the time, but painful. Later on, however, it produces a harvest of righteousness and peace for those trained by it .(Hebrews 12:11, NIV)

One of the keys to good discipline is anticipating what might happen in advance and developing strategies to stop it ever happening.

Below is a list of possible disruptive behaviours. Write them on separate pieces of paper and rate them on a scale 1 to 10 with 1 being very serious and 10 being a mild problem.

1   Not joining in an organised activity.
2   Eating sweets at the back and sharing them with neighbours.
3   Shouting at another group member during group time.
4   Talking while you are.
5   Fighting with a member of the group.
6   Breaking a piece of furniture.
7   Getting a fit of the giggles.
8   Drawing on the handout you gave them.
9   Distracting others by drawing attention to themselves.
10 Tickling the person next to them.
11 Stealing from someone.
12 Making a paper aeroplane and throwing it during the talk.

Now try to group them into piles according to how serious they are.

What would be an appropriate action to take as discipline for each of these examples? Which issues would require you to talk to parents?

Chat with other group leaders to make sure that you come up with a consistent approach.

If you had to decide on a minimum set of rules, how many would there be and what would they be?

Can you condense these into some principles, eg leaders sitting amongst the group of young people rather than together as a group will enable discipline issues to be dealt with more easily.

The better our relationships with young people, the more likely we are to anticipate the signs of trouble.

Child Protection

Every week there seem to be stories in the paper about the mistreatment of children by adults whom they trusted. As adults working with young people in the church context we need to act responsibly and be aware of legislation. We also need to be exemplary in our behaviour and conduct with young people. All that we do should both reflect and promote good practice for all those entrusted to our care.

Legislation

At a very basic level this means that we should take seriously the whole framework of legislation for anyone working with children and young people. All those who have unsupervised contact with young people need to have an Enhanced Disclosure clearance from the Criminal Records Bureau. We also need to be aware of appropriate ratios of adults to young people for supervision. But it does not only apply to this area. There is legislation concerning use of premises: making sure that they are safe, that fire exits are clearly labelled. If you take young people on any outdoor activity then there is a licensing arrangement for outdoor activity providers and legislation concerning which activities need to be licensed. It is your responsibility to make sure that what you are doing complies with the law. There are particular issues about what to do if a young person discloses to you that they are the victim of some form of abuse. Your church should have a clear procedure about what to do and all those involved in the children's and youth work should know what to do.

Parental permission

Young people would like to be independent from their parents but we cannot act in ways that ignore the fact that they're still dependent. We need to be completely transparent about our activities with young people. Keeping parents informed and being accountable to them is a vital part of good practice. If you have a regular programme of activities then get parents to complete a permission form when the young person joins the group, including some basic questions about any healthcare needs or allergies, eg do they have any special needs, receive regular medication or have any disabilities that we should be aware? Are they allergic to anything? (Nut allergies particularly important here.)

The parental permission form should also authorise you to act in an emergency. For any special events, make sure that you have outlined exactly what activities you are going to do and the level of supervision involved.

Policies and procedures

Appropriate behaviour and expectations for leaders need to be clear. The best way to achieve that is to have a comprehensive set of policies to cover different situations. There are particular issues about physical contact with young people, inappropriate relationships between young people and leaders, appropriate one-to-one contact situations, health and safety issues including first aid. The more help and guidance we can give, the better we are supporting the leaders of groups.

Child protection

The issues of child protection are in the public eye so it is important to take this very seriously. If you are part of a denomination or a network of churches then start by asking them for advice. Alternatively there are a wide range of organisations who act in this area.

Churches Child Protection Advisory Service (CCPAS)
- http://www.ccpas.co.uk
- Churches agency for safeguarding http://www.churchsafe.org.uk
- Amaze http://www.amaze.org.uk

Denominational agencies
- Baptists: http://www.baptist.org.uk
- United Reformed Church: http://www.urc.org.uk
- Methodists: http://www.methodist.org.uk
- Assemblies of God: http://www.aog.org.uk

Make sure all leaders apply for an enhanced disclosure. Check out details on http://www.disclosure.gov.uk

Data protection

If you keep information on paper or electronically about young people or leaders, they have the right to see it. Check out the law on data protection:

http://www.informationcommissioner.gov.uk

Health and safety

You should make sure that your insurance policy covers you for off-site activities and that you operate safe procedures. The DfES has a good section on school visits, many of which could apply to us:

http://dfes,gov.uk/h_s_ev/index,shtml

Good practice

The youth and children's section of the Evangelical Alliance has some good links to examples of good practice:

www.eauk.org/Contentmanager/Content/youthandchildren/promotinggoodpractice.cfm

Song words

If you are going to project, copy or write out the words of songs you need a licence from Christian Copyright Licensing International. http://www.ccli.co.uk

Personal integrity

We want all those who work with young people to act in ways that show integrity. But it is easy to forget that young people are experiencing a period of massive change. It is all too easy for girls to have a crush on young male leaders or for young people to develop a strong attachment to one of the leaders in the group. It can be easy to be flattered by this attention and, because we have stressed the importance of relationships, to misread the signs. Think carefully about how what you say and do might be misunderstood – taking care that all that you do and say is in an open and seen environment. Working in a team should provide both support and accountability – be willing to listen to others and examine how your behaviour might be seen or perceived.

All of these guidelines serve a two-fold purpose:

1   To protect the young people in our care so that what we do for them is the safest and best it can be.
2   To protect the leaders from inappropriate behaviour or placing themselves at risk of allegations or breaking the law.

Managing a group

So this is it! You've planned, put all your policies in place, got all your equipment ready and you are raring to go. At the door are 30 young people – noisy and full of energy. How will you manage to cope with them and make this and subsequent weeks significant times of growth for these young disciples?

Group dynamics

It's amazing how differently people behave as part of a large group. You need to recognise this and look at ways of engendering a sense of belonging. As young people feel that they belong, they will begin to grow in confidence and their real character will show. You will have the extroverts and the shy, the academic and the sporty, the thinkers and the action orientated. Learning to handle the group means looking for ways for everyone to contribute.

So think in advance about how to draw out the quiet members and how to channel the enthusiasm of the lively characters. In your conversations listen out for talents and skills you can employ. Remember that if you always ask for volunteers you will always get the same people. Ask some in advance who might not volunteer.

In a similar way think about how you place people in groups. Young people are much more likely to be comfortable with their friends, so separating them is likely to make it more difficult for some members to share. The way that some group members relate to each other might lead to you keep them apart – they argue or act silly – but you want it to be a place they enjoy coming to, so don't treat it like school.

Handling your group

Young people come in all shapes and sizes. Below is a range of roles that young people play in a group.

The Intellectual: Every discussion needs to be at a higher level. They will introduce ideas into the discussion that were never intended or needed, interpret others' words and read into what others say. Useful on occasions but might make others feel inferior.

The Joker: Messes around, makes jokes and keeps everyone laughing. They help reduce tension and stop us taking ourselves too seriously. But they can also be a disruption and make others feel intimidated.

The Encourager: Draws others out, worries about how people feel, keeps people talking and helps the group to be a pleasant experience for all. A group in which everyone was like this might just find it difficult to really engage with any issues.

The Withdrawn: Doesn't want to be here and wants everyone to know it. They look bored, don't talk and stare into space. If they draw others into their behaviour they can stop the group functioning.

The Thoughtful: Some people are simply quiet by nature and its easy to assume they aren't interested when they are simply shy. Struggling to talk in the group, they nevertheless have things to offer.

The Talker: Some people can't stand silence and this group member is fast to talk and slow to listen. Always first to give an answer, they often speak before thinking and stop others from participating.

The Nurse: Thinks that all disagreement is a bad thing and simply wants everyone to be happy. They stop conflict but go so far that the group can't disagree about anything.

Discuss how you would make sure these members contributed to your group. What pitfalls are there? What specific action would you take?

Team working

A group of leaders working together in a group need to act as a team. Any team will function better if the members know each other. You will need to meet to plan and evaluate so that the group runs well. But you will function better if there are other occasions when you meet up too. What about meeting up socially once a term and meeting to pray on a regular basis? As you get to know each other you will be able to encourage one another, share joys and pains, and rejoice together in what God is doing through you. One way of achieving this would be to have an away day together with a mixture of relaxation, prayer, training and vision building. When you all know what you are hoping to achieve you will be able to work together more effectively.

Raising the profile

Your group does not exist in isolation. It is part of the ministry of your church. Looking for ways of reflecting that and building a higher profile will help young people to make that connection. Some ways to do this:

- Have a notice board with details of your activities, regularly updated with new photos.
- List all your activities in the church diary or notice sheet.
- Produce a regular parents update of what you are doing.
- Arrange special events to which parents can come, and other church members too.
- Participate in services so that your group members are seen and not just at special services.
- Get people to pray for the group as part of the church service, the prayer meeting or in house/home groups.

Raising the profile like this will help the group integrate into the church family. It will also give people a glimpse of what is involved in being a leader and make it easier to recruit future leaders.

Enjoy it

If we want the young people to have fun, then we need to enjoy the work too. It is important that we keep our enthusiasm fresh. Young people can tell if we feel compelled to attend and they will be able to read those indicators.

- Attend training events to get new ideas and sharpen your skills.
- Read books to challenge your thinking.
- Try out new ideas on a regular basis – look for ways to improve them and use them again.
- Don't stick with the same programme all the time – vary the mix.
- Laugh about the things that go wrong and celebrate the things that go well.

Your enthusiasm is a vital part of your investment in the faith development of these young people. Remember – long after they remember what you said, they will remember the sort of person you were.

Resources

Scripture Union: http://www.scriptureunion.org.uk
TheGRID is the curriculum material for 11–14s, produced every quarter and containing 13 (or 14) flexible, easy-to-use session outlines, enough for three months if you get together each week. It includes Photocopiable pages and an integrated CD-ROM containing animated and video presentations, printable resource sheets, music and much more, access to further resources, downloads, training and information on the GRID website.

Check out http://www.scriptureunion.org.uk/light/thegridoverview.asp
Also check out the main Scripture Union website for other group resources for 11–14s.

Youth for Christ: http://www.yfc.co.uk
Rock Solid: Help for churches wanting to set up and run a Rock Solid Club in their area. http://www.yfc.co.uk/Youth_Leaders/church_resources/#rocksolid

Rock Solid 2: follow on to Rock Solid aimed at groups of Christian young people.
http://www.yfc.co.uk/Youth_Leaders/church_resources/#RS2

Crusaders: http://www.crusaders.org.uk
Encounters of a Lifetime – Nine sessions based on a TV 'magazine style' format, focusing on people who met Jesus... and on those who still meet with him today! ISBN 1 897987 12 9

What's in it for me? Ten sessions to help young people discover God's Word for themselves. Discussion based with lots of photocopiable visual aids.
ISBN 1 897987 22 6

Christian Camping International: http://www.cci.org.uk
If you are looking for a venue for a weekend away for your group, check out the venue finder facility from CCI/UK.

CPAS: www.cpas.org.uk
Check out the CPAS website for resources for ministry with young people.

Chapter Nine – Growing Church

The importance of belonging

Growing disciples need the support of a believing community. Nurture of faith by believing adults throughout childhood is important for long-term commitment to Christ. In the rollercoaster years of early adolescence, the support of good relationships is essential if 11–14s are to continue growing in faith as they grow in maturity.

Yet, this model of faith nurture, if dependent on a local church, often cannot work. For some 11–14s, Sunday morning church just doesn't fit easily with their lives. Then, many 'churched' 11–14s are simply choosing not to belong to a church once the drive towards independence has kicked in. Recent research by Peter Brierley suggests that a thousand under-15s were leaving the church each week through the nineties, and, more recently, that the key time for early adolescents to leave the church is at the end of Junior school[1].

Twelve-year-old Luke has grown tall recently. He's beginning to enjoy a regular social life on Saturday evenings with his non-Christian friends. Sunday mornings has always meant church. But now he certainly doesn't feel very comfortable with the same old children's group activities he's been doing for years. He hates being treated as if he's a little kid. Why does he need to go to church anyway? What's it for? He decides to tell his parents that he's not going any more.

11–14s are at a peak time for stopping going to church; they're also, developmentally, at a key time in their search for meaning, identity and for growing commitment to faith. If they're not part of a local congregation, how can they be given the ongoing nurture and support necessary for faith growth? If they leave, they may not come back.

It's an urgent issue. How can we make our local expression of 'church' a more comfortable place for 11–14s, so that they want to stay (or even to come in for the first time)?

The big question of how faith communities develop and find expression in the present time might seem a discouraging one. Alternatively, we can see it as an exciting challenge as we watch God's transforming work and respond to his Spirit.

The 'problem' of church

Practical issues

Society has changed and that has inevitably had an impact on whether 11–14s can easily come to a church meeting on Sunday mornings. Think about the following, together with the questions on page 149.

Being church...

How do the following ideas help your thinking about being church with 11–14s?

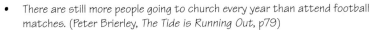

- There are still more people going to church every year than attend football matches. (Peter Brierley, *The Tide is Running Out*, p79)

- Research for the past few decades has consistently shown that church attendance declines as young people enter adolescence. Recently, the age at which this seems to be happening is earlier, possibly reflecting earlier onset of adolescence, growing independence, changing parental and family situations.

- The figures for adults in their thirties and forties, the age group likely to be parents of 11–14s, also show an increasing decline in church attendance (*Tide*, p101). This lack of parental church commitment undoubtedly has an effect on the involvement of their children.

- Not wishing to be part of institutional church does not necessarily indicate a young person's loss of belief or faith. They may be involved in a variety of other Christian activities with different 'believing communities' not associated with one particular local church.

- The research figures from Peter Brierley's study reflect Sunday church attendance figures, not attendance at midweek activities (*Tide*, p97). So, it may be that the decline in church attendance figures is not as great as first feared.

- Most young people are not concerned about commitment to one particular denomination.

- The local church is only one expression of the kingdom of God. Members of God's kingdom are united across denominations, history, national and racial boundaries. The rule of God is active by his Spirit in his world – in situations and in the lives of people not yet touched by local expressions of church.

Sources include:

Peter Brierley, *The Tide is Running Out*; Peter Brierley, *Reaching and Keeping Tweenagers*

- Society generally has no expectation of Sunday church attendance. Sunday church was established in a time when 'everyone' went to church. Today's supporting culture for 11–14s does not include expectation of church attendance.
- Families move. The established models for church attendance began in a time when people were likely to stay in one community for all of their lives and when transport to your local church meant walking. Young people today move with their families, are new to a town, are looking for friends, are dependent on others for travel to church.
- There are other Sunday options. When society thought of itself as 'Christian', everything stopped on Sundays, and 'church' was one social activity you could, and were expected to, take part in. 11–14s today are faced with a whole range of other options, expectations and obligations, for example:

Options: shopping, watching TV, playing electronic games, cinema, special events, big sports events, staying in bed.

Expectations: school football matches, drama rehearsals, music events, friends' parties and sleepovers.

Obligations: seeing the 'other' parent for the weekend; parents are working, so unable to transport their 11 to 14-year-old to church; seeing family in another part of the country (11–14s are becoming independent, but still are largely dependent on adults' choices); homework.

But it's not only practical considerations and issues of contemporary culture which put 11–14s off being part of a local church community. Sometimes, it's just not a place where they feel comfortable.

Changing the culture

Many 11–14s find 'church' an alien culture. Adults seem to wear special kinds of clothes, use a special kind of language (not just formal liturgy), have special rules about when you can or can't speak; and the physical setting is often uncomfortable. The old 'school model' of church – with the congregation sitting in rows facing the front, and expected to sit without talking to others for at least an hour, concentrating on whatever is being said from the front, with no opportunity for commenting or asking questions – is alien to 11–14s, both developmentally and to their experience of life outside of church (eg interactive teaching at school; interactive electronic media; short time-span activities with TV and web). The cerebral nature of church with its physically passive focus on text medium is unsuited to many 11–14s and alien to their world. In *Reaching and Keeping Tweenagers*, Peter Brierley's research findings underline that 11–14s are not happy with formality[2]. They want a more relaxed atmosphere, where it's OK to wear what you like, sit comfortably, talk and enjoy meeting with others.

More important than buildings, entertaining programmes or expensive equipment – whatever the faith community activity – the key factor is relationships. Whether or not we think it's a good enough reason, peer group friendships at church are a major reason why younger adolescents stay. The lack of other young people of the same age, and unfriendliness from adults, is a major reason why they leave.

Sunday church...

Use the questions below to help you think/talk about solutions to these obstacles for 11–14s' involvement in church:

*   No expectation of Sunday church attendance

    How can we create a counter-expectation which makes meeting together with other Christians an exciting and unmissable occasion for 11–14s? Is there a better time for them (and adults?) to meet?

*   Families move

    Is our church/our 11–14s group welcoming? How are we helping 'new' young people to integrate? How can we help address transport problems? Are we looking out for those who have just moved into our area?

*   Other Sunday choices

    How can we disciple this age group when they may often be unable to attend a Sunday or weekend meeting regularly? Here's one example:

    Laura's away from home every other weekend at her dad's. She's part of a cell group which meets during the week, led by one of the older young people in her church. Her group leader keeps in touch by email in the week, asking how the visit to her dad went and telling her any info she missed. The group all use MSN anyway — exchanging prayer news and sharing their common concerns as young Christians.

How far do we recognise the difficulties 11–14s may have in 'coming to church'? Could you make a midweek evening the main time for teaching instead of a Sunday morning group?

Like on *The Simpsons?*

Overheard, between two friends (boys, one Christian, one non-Christian, aged 11–14) one Sunday lunchtime:

Non-Christian friend: 'So where've you been this morning?'

Christian: 'Church.'

Non-Christian friend: 'What's that?'

Christian: 'You know... like on *The Simpsons.*'

Non-Christian: 'Oh.'

Whose church?

Well, Christ's, of course. But it doesn't always look, or feel, like that for young people, and perhaps especially for 11–14s who, whilst growing in their adult perceptions and judgements, often have no recognised voice or power (unlike older youth groups in some churches). It's the adults up front – often male, middle-class, white, well-educated, materially well-off (and possibly reasonably good-looking and musically-gifted!) – who seem to run the show. Of course, it doesn't matter what the social background or culture of a leader is, but it does matter if that particular culture or style gets confused with the way things ought to be – for ever. If 11–14s feel that church is the province of a certain kind of adult, then they will feel excluded from the body of Christ. They need to know that they are valued. The adults upfront are servants of Christ. His dynamic, believing community rests on his work and words.

So, how can we obey his words and 'Love each other' (John 15:17, NIV) when it comes to 11–14s?

Minding the gap[3]

The 'children's work' at church often includes young people up to the age of 14. Then, if still part of church, those young people move into the youth group or attend the 'adult' service. Today, as discussed in previous chapters, 11–14s are moving into adolescence, with all its associated changes, earlier. School, TV and advertising all recognise this age group's growing maturity and aspirations to independence. Adult Christians often don't. Whilst church structures are beginning to acknowledge this, 11–14s are still sometimes left feeling patronised. They know they have stepped beyond their childhood world.

At secondary school and coping with the onset of puberty, they know they are not just the oldest of the 'children's' groups. Equally, it may be felt that they are not mature enough to cope with the more socially independent, older young people, who, for their part, may feel uncomfortable with 11–14s. However, if this age group feel patronised and uncomfortable in the children's department, and are also unwelcome in the 'youth group', there is a gap. More than this, the potential of this stage for spiritual development may be missed, as their questions and developing gifts are not expressed.

Martin Saunders[4] makes the point that those working with young people in churches tend to be either children's workers or working with 'youth' (which often means 14+). There is sometimes no awareness of the need for special focus on this 'New Youth' age group, which is tailored for their needs and spiritual development. Of course, man- or woman-power is often a problem in churches. Who will do this work? But at least, if church structures take seriously the particular needs of 11–14s, and adults in the congregation learn to treat them in ways which acknowledge their increasing maturity, then relationships may develop which support their faith journey as they become young adults who continue to participate in the worshipping life of the church.

Biblical pictures of church

- Matthew 16:18 – the church belongs to Christ.
- John 10:1–21; John 21:15–19 – Jesus is the good Shepherd, his disciples the flock.
- Colossians 3:12–14 - A community of 'virtues', with love as the key.
- Matthew 7:24–27 – a community founded on obedience to the words of Jesus.
- 1 Peter 2:4–10; 1 Corinthians 3:11 – a building in progress, dependent on Jesus as the 'cornerstone' or 'foundation'.
- Romans 12:3–8 – a body with many different parts which make up the whole.
- Revelation 19:6–8 – a bride being prepared for the wedding day.

Some of these verses are speaking about 'local' church, some are more about worldwide-and-throughout history church. Either way, what issues do they raise for how we are working with 11–14s in church? Here are some questions to get you thinking about ideas in these Bible verses:

- Is your work with 11–14s founded on Jesus and his teaching?

- How well does the picture of looking after sheep (for the Shepherd), fit with your work with 11–14s?

- How are the gifts, abilities, words and understandings of 11–14s acknowledged and used for the good of others in your group and in your church?

- How central to your work with 11–14s is the idea of transformation?

- How loving are relationships with your group – between themselves, you and the wider church?

Intergenerational matters...

The advent of 'youth culture' (see Chapter Three) in the mid-twentieth century contributed to the expansion of youth ministry in the church, for mid and older teenagers at least. A downside of this for church has been that 'youth culture' has resulted in a distancing between older and younger people, resulting in frustration for the young, loss for the older generation, and missed opportunity for mission.

Unlike the world's 'story' of only valuing the here-and-now, the Christian faith story learns from the past to find direction for living now, as it looks forward to the future. (This idea is explored in challenging books by David Bosch[5] and Walter Brueggemann[6].)

> *God gave his Law to Jacob's descendants, the people of Israel. And he told our ancestors to teach their children, so that each new generation would know his Law and tell it to the next. Then they would trust God and obey his teachings, without forgetting anything God had done. (Psalm 78:5–7)*

All generations are needed in Christian community. How will young people learn and understand if they are not taught by older people? How will younger people, shaped by today's culture, hear the message unless it is proclaimed in the words and ways of today?

Single generation church models may be an easy option for both young and older people, and may fulfil a temporary gap, the result of the rapid cultural transition our society is undergoing. (See Graham Cray, *Postmodern Culture and Youth Discipleship*[7], for more discussion of this idea.) However, young people don't stay young. What then? And older people need the energy and care of young people. Unlike non-Christian society's tendency to search out people who are 'just like me', Christ's church embraces diversity (Galatians 3:28): Jew, Gentile, men, women, slave, free... adult, older teenager, 11 to 14-year-old, child... and challenges us to accept one another and find ways of learning from each other about Christ, and how to serve him – together.

Give them a voice

11–14s pick up the unspoken messages from adults in church. For example: is there a sense of 'now the *real* worship can begin', as they leave the adult congregation for their teaching groups? Do adults give them the impression that they are 'non-persons'. Although asked, do adults really take their points of view seriously on church matters? And, if their sense of personal relationship with God is growing, do they have permission to voice their perceptions of Christ and his message?

It's not that they do not need the support of adults, or that they do not need teaching. It's not a case of 'anything goes' and that a diverse range of very young people can do anything they like. But their voices do need to be valued. Participation must be more than token. Being given responsibility affirms their value and brings a sense of ownership, both of faith and church: they are 'house members' not 'house guests'[8].

These are things we learnt from our ancestors, and we will tell them to the next generation. (Psalm 78:3,4)

Authority or control?

Allowing 11–14s to have a voice might sound risky – but it doesn't mean giving up sensible boundary-setting or care for young people whose experience of life and God are limited. 'Loving one another' includes respect for each other and relating to one another in age-appropriate ways.

Look again at some of the Bible adolescents mentioned in Chapter One:

Jesus (Luke 2:41–51); Samuel (1 Samuel 2,3); Esther (Esther)

Also look at:

David (1 Samuel 16,17); Josiah (2 Kings 22,23; 2 Chronicles 34,35)

- Each of these young people had a significant part to play in God's plan and purposes.

- They were able to grow in their relationship with God or take action for him because of the acknowledgement of adults around them that God was at work in their lives.

- Their actions were essential for the good of God's people.

- None of them was alone. Each had older, more experienced, faithful mentors. In the case of Jesus and Samuel they continued from their early youth to grow in faith and develop under the authority of their adult carers.

- You have a key role in investing in the lives of the young people you work with!

The greatest in the kingdom…

'I tell you the truth, unless you change and become like little children, you will never enter the kingdom of heaven … And whoever welcomes a little child like this in my name welcomes me.' (Matthew 18:3,5, NIV)

Take a look at Matthew 18:1–6.

Using Jesus' words to help you think about 11–14s who are growing in faith, what might it suggest about how we listen to them and nurture their belief in Jesus?

Growing communities

Many different models for church are emerging as God's people respond imaginatively to changing times and particular situations. For this book, the important thing is, that as adults find new ways of being church, they continue to nurture children and young people, so that they too are helped to grow into independent faith.

Some ways of working with 11–14s were considered in Chapter Six and some biblical pictures of church earlier in this chapter. Here's a summary of some key elements and possible models for growing Christian community which include 11–14s:

Key elements

- Working with 11–14s in church is not just about giving them knowledge. It's about helping them know God personally. Faith is learnt as it is experienced.
- All-age church doesn't mean that all ages always meet only together – with no one group's needs ever being met. Believing community will include different groups meeting at different times, but with all knowing they are equally valued as a vital part of the body.
- There will be times when intergenerational community does gather together. It's important that 11–14s experience times with adults of Bible learning, prayer, worship. Think about how these help 11–14s see that older people are dependent on God and in relationship with him.
- Relationships with others are key – for a sense of belonging, for faith growth. No one can go it alone.
- The church is Christ's church. It is about relationship with God, made possible through Jesus. It's about being transformed as we serve him together and are obedient to his Word. Are we helping 11–14s know that this is what we're about?

Ideas for growing communities

- Sunday morning might be a regular time for the whole church meeting together, but perhaps midweek or another time at the weekend is better for your group of 11–14s.
- If your group has its learning time whilst adults are meeting too, include some worship, prayer and Bible time together with the adults first. When the age groups separate for different teaching groups, make sure that 11–14s don't feel that they are being sent out with the children. For example, Scripture Union's learning material *theGRID* is especially designed for this age group, recognising that they are young 'youth', not children. (How about the adults leaving the main meeting room some times?)
- Read the Bible (leaders and 11–14s), to learn from it together. Resources like *Word Up* provide short 20–25 minute outlines including a fun starter activity, some ways into the Bible verses and ideas for application and prayer.
- Encourage young people to be in a prayer partnership or to organise and be part of a prayer triplet.
- School groups. School is their world. Teacher-led or pupil-led, whether mainly for mission or mainly for faith support – a Christian school group can play an important part in nurturing their faith. As with peer-led cell groups, the young people themselves must take responsibility for involvement and leadership.

Cells for 11–14s

- Peer-led might seem ambitious with 11–14s, but it can work with some of the older ones leading a group of younger people. Provide strong support, including help with preparation, feedback time and prayer. The young cell group leaders will need their own cell group.

- Alternatively, invite slightly older teenagers to be cell group leaders or mentors for this age group.

- When, where, how long? This age group have lots to do (homework, music practice), prefer short time slots, are dependent for transport on parents who won't want them travelling home independently after dark. So, maybe in your home – or in one of theirs, which could be more relaxed, but might not be if there is competition with younger brothers and sisters, television etc.

- Or, you could include cell group time within all-together church time, or at a youth meeting time, which includes a time for cell groups. This way, the more-focused thinking about faith takes place within the context of relaxed atmosphere and relationships.

- Cell groups – peer-led or slightly older teenager-led – can be a great way of helping young Christians take responsibility and of training them as leaders. If it is a 'youth' cell group, it will help all the members in their developing sense of ownership of faith and of their church.

Find out more:

Phil Potter, *The Challenge of Cell Church*, BRF, 2001

Graham Cray, *Youth Congregations and the Emerging Church*, Grove Books Ltd, 2002

Liz West, *Young People in Cells – the Challenge to the Church*, Anvil, 15,4,1998

- Networking. 11–14s aren't just involved in one Christian community. They may be part of many different Christian groups and networks. Encourage this sense of identity with members of God's kingdom, acknowledging the impact that those networks are having on 'your' 11 to 14-year-olds, for example: a group of Christians at school, Christian friends made at last year's Christian holiday or event, email and web groups.

Church and 11–14s

Supporting 11–14s

Working with 11–14s, as previous chapters make clear, is not just about how their group is run for an hour each week. Whilst 11–14s may have their own special leaders, their faith is nurtured by the whole of the church. Here are some ways that everyone can help:

- The modelling of faith and love for Christ and his Word in what we do and say.
- Trusting and secure relationships. This takes time and commitment.
- Allowing and encouraging conversation about faith matters – exploration of questions, doubts, beliefs – within the context of believing relationships.
- Recognise and respect the growing maturity of the young person.
- Entrusting with responsibility in some area of church community life. Not just token occasional 'youth group' participation, but allowing them to make a real contribution to every area of church life.
- Allow opportunities for 11–14s to use their gifts.
- Pray for them. Could different adults in the congregation commit themselves to pray for one particular young person as they pass through this stage of life?
- Older people/older young people can offer to be 'mentors', or just be willing to offer friendship and a chance to chat. Or be willing to be the extra person needed in the meeting room or on a trip out to fulfil your Church's Child Protection Policy.
- Practicalities: subsidising activities; attendance at events; Christian holidays; buying of Bibles, Bible notes, song books and equipment; offering hospitality, food and lifts.

Support for leaders

11–14s are at a crucial stage for faith development. Recognition and understanding of the significant, but difficult, role of the leader is important.

- Talk to your church leadership team about why 11–14s are such a significant age group.
- Ask for opportunities to talk to the church about your group.
- Look for leaders who are committed to working with this age group, rather than with 14+ or children.
- Look for leaders who can give the time needed for building good relationships.
- Keep the church informed of what the 11–14s are doing, their needs and any ways in which the rest of the church can help.
- Ask for prayer support from the church for your ministry with the young people.
- Talk/share ideas with others working with the church's young people, even if their age group isn't 11–14s.
- Pray for one another.

Using the Net...

Email, MSN, web interactive sites, texting are 'owned' by the age group. Faith and beliefs will be owned too, expressed in words appropriate to the medium and their generation, without adult control.

Electronic media are strengthening existing networks of Christians as well as creating online faith communities. Both can help build a young person's sense of identity with other believers.

Use emails, MSN and texting for communication of information, prayer and praise requests, sharing cares, concerns, encouragements and devotional Bible material. The 'anytime, anywhere, every day' nature of this communication means 11–14s can have a sense of being part of their believing community wherever they are and a sense of God's care through the week.

Websites. Interactive 'online' communities can provide another way of experiencing being part of God's family. Take a look at www.scriptureunion.org.uk/oneup or www.grid-online.org

How does the Net help?

Q: In what ways do you use the Net?

Jo: MSN mainly – we all exchanged our Hotmail addresses at the holiday I've been going to for the last few years. There's a message board on the holiday's website too. Mainly, I just talk to people when I'm on the computer and I see they're online too.

Q: How does using the Net help you as a Christian?

Jo: It helps me have real friendships which carry on with the people I met who I might not see for a whole year otherwise. We can exchange news and help each other with problems.

Q: Is it good way of feeling supported in your faith?

Jo: Yes – because you can ask questions – especially to leaders – and get support from them and your friends. With online conversations, there's time to think about what you want to say and to think about people's answers.

More ideas for leader support...

- Talk about programming and event planning with others in the church. Watch out that your programme doesn't clash with what other age groups are doing, or facilities and equipment others are expecting to use at the same time.

- Parents know their 11 to 14-year-old very well. Christian parents are workers with you in the faith nurture of their child. Make use of their knowledge, listen to their concerns, enlist their help (when not too embarrassing for their children!). Pray together.

- Get some training support. This might be a formal course which your youth and children's team go to, or you could do something home-grown using this book.

- Make sure you are getting challenged and nurtured in your own faith and relationship with Jesus. You can't give to them unless you are receiving too. Be part of teaching times when you are not leading the group. Pray and read the Bible with adults. Read magazines like *Youthwork* or a journal like *Journal of Youth and Theology* both to give you new ideas and a sense of community and support from others working with young people. Watch out for national and local youth training events.

God's kingdom will grow!

It's a special and privileged calling to work with this age group – although it might not always feel like that! But every so often, God gives us glimpses of his transforming work in their lives.

Today is a special time. We are being challenged about church and our witness to the world. Things are changing and Christ is transforming his church. Believing community is emerging in all kinds of surprising places and ways.

Jesus said:

> The kingdom of heaven is like a mustard seed, which a man took and planted in his field. Though it is the smallest of all your seeds, yet when it grows, it is the largest of garden plants and becomes a tree, so that the birds of the air come and perch in its branches. (Matthew 13:31,32, NIV)

God's life, once planted, grows.

If you had any doubts before, we hope this book will have encouraged you and confirmed your belief that those of us who work with 11–14s are playing a significant role in God's kingdom. So, the next time you think your group time has been an unintended riot, or the boys just look bored for the whole of your teaching session, or the girls have spent the evening doing their hair or talking about boys, or all your carefully made plans didn't work because only one person came… don't give up! You could be investing in someone as sold out for God as Samuel, Esther, David or Josiah… And the impact of that on our culture could be awesome!

More biblical models for church

Exodus – Joshua: *God's people journey together.*

Nehemiah 8: *the gathered community listens, learns, repents and celebrates together.*

Acts 2:42-47: *the early church learns, reflects, prays, shares, praises and witnesses together.*

1 Corinthians: *problems in the early church.*

1 Timothy; 1 John: *learning to live as believing communities.*

Look back at the biblical models for church on page 151 too.

References for Chapter Nine

1   Peter Brierley, *Reaching and Keeping Tweenagers*, pp3,7

2   Peter Brierley, ibid

3   Martin Saunders, 'Mind the gap!', *Youthwork* magazine, May 2003

4   Martin Saunders, ibid

5   David J Bosch, *Transforming Mission*

6   Walter Brueggemann, *Texts Under Negotiation*

7   Graham Cray, *Postmodern Culture and Youth Discipleship*, p24

8   Tim Van Meter and Katherine Turpin, 'No Longer Guests', *Journal of Youth and Theology*, Nov 2002, p17

...and further reading

David Hilborn and Matt Bird (eds), *God and the Generations*

Pete Ward, *Liquid Church*

Church House Publishing, *Mission-shaped Church*

Peter Brierley, *Reaching and Keeping Tweenagers*

Francis Bridger, *Children Finding Faith*

John H Westerhoff III, *Will Our Children Have Faith?*

Peter Brierley, *The Tide is Running Out*

Peter Brierley, *Steps to the Future*

William Kay and Leslie Francis, *Drift from the Churches*

Bibliography

Jeff Astley (ed), *How faith grows: Faith development and Christian education*, The National Society and Church House Publishing, 1991

Jenny Baker, 'Tweenage Kids' and 'Growing Pains', in *Youthwork* magazine, January 2003 and February 2003

David J Bosch, *Transforming Mission: Paradigm Shifts in Theology of Mission*, Orbis Books, 1996

Francis Bridger, *Children Finding Faith*, Scripture Union and CPAS, 2000

Peter Brierley, *Steps to the Future: Issues facing the church in the new millennium*, Christian Research and Scripture Union, 2000

Peter Brierley, *The Tide is Running Out*, Christian Research, 2000

Peter Brierley, *Reaching and Keeping Tweenagers: Analysis of the 2001 RAKES Survey*, Christian Research, 2002

Walter Brueggemann, *Texts Under Negotiation: The Bible and Postmodern Imagination*, Fortress Press, 1993

Church House Publishing, *Mission-shaped Church: Church Planting and Fresh Expressions of Church in a Changing Context*, 2004

Terry Clutterham, *The Adventure Begins*, Scripture Union and CPAS, 1996

Graham Cray, *Postmodern Culture and Youth Discipleship: Commitment or Looking Cool?*, Grove Books, 1998

Steven Croft, *Transforming Communities*, Darton, Longman & Todd Ltd, 2002

Ken Edgecombe, *Will they or won't they?*, Scripture Union, 2000

Paul Fenton, '*Youthwork Policy Paper*', Scripture Union, internal document

Paul Fenton, *Someone to Lean On: Accompanying Young People on the Journey of Faith*, Scripture Union, 1998

Doug Fields, *Purpose-Driven Youth Ministry*, Zondervan, 1998

James Fowler, *Stages of Faith*, Harper and Row, 1981

Leslie Francis, *The Values Debate: A Voice from the Pupils*, Woburn Press, 2001

Barrie Gunter and Adrian Furnham, *Children as Consumers*, Routledge, 1998

John Head, *Working with Adolescents: Constructing Identity*, The Falmer Press, 1997

David Hilborn and Matt Bird (eds), *God and the Generations: Youth, Age and the Church Today*, Paternoster Press, 2002

John Hull, 'Spiritual Development: Interpretations and Applications', *British Journal of Religious Education*, Summer 2002, 24:3, p171–182

Stephen D Jones, *Faith Shaping: Youth and the Experience of Faith*, Judson Press, 1987

William Kay and Leslie Francis, *Drift from the Churches: Attitude towards Christianity During Childhood and Adolescence*, University of Wales Press, 1996

Richard Middleton and Brian Walsh, *Truth is Stranger than it Used to Be: Biblical Faith in a Postmodern Age*, SPCK, 1995

Jolyon P Mitchell, *Visually Speaking: Radio and the Renaissance of Preaching*, T&T Clark, 1999

Lesslie Newbigin, *The Gospel in a Pluralist Society*, SPCK, 1989

Claire Pedrick and Andy Morgan, *Friends First?*, Scripture Union, 2002

Claire Pedrick and Andy Morgan, *Under Pressure*, Scripture Union, 2004

Martin Saunders, 'Mind the gap!', *Youthwork*, May 2003

Tom and Christine Sine, *Living on Purpose*, Monarch Books, 2002

Don Tapscott, *Growing Up Digital: The Rise of the Net Generation*, McGraw-Hill, 1999

Tim Van Meter and Katherine Turpin, 'No Longer Guests', *Journal of Youth and Theology*, Nov 2002

Pete Ward, *Youth Culture and the Gospel*, Marshall Pickering, 1992

Pete Ward, *Liquid Church*, Paternoster Press, 2002

John H Westerhoff III, *Will our Children have Faith?*, Morehouse Publishing, 2000